EQUITABLE CHOICES FOR HEALTH

JOE FARRINGTON-DOUGLAS AND JESSICA ALLEN

ippr

The **Institute for Public Policy Research** (ippr) is the UK's leading progressive think tank and was established in 1988. Its role is to bridge the political divide between the social democratic and liberal traditions, the intellectual divide between academia and the policy making establishment and the cultural divide between government and civil society. It is first and foremost a research institute, aiming to provide innovative and credible policy solutions. Its work, the questions its research poses and the methods it uses are driven by the belief that the journey to a good society is one that places social justice, democratic participation and economic and environmental sustainability at its core.

For further information you can contact ippr's external affairs department on info@ippr.org, you can view our website at www.ippr.org and you can buy our books from Central Books on 0845 458 9910 or email ippr@centralbooks.com.

Our trustees

CONTENTS

Executive summary

Progressive vision of equitable choices

Choice is at the heart of the government's public service reform agenda. In healthcare, patients will be offered new choices, not only in choosing a hospital but also, increasingly in primary care. This report argues for a progressive vision of choice in healthcare, where disadvantaged patients are empowered to make choices throughout their care, to reduce healthcare inequities and tackle health inequalities. Choice should aim to do more than create a market. The primary goal of choice should be to improve outcomes and reduce inequalities.

At present, government policy on patient choice risks worsening inequities in healthcare. However, removing choice would also sustain current inequities whereby middle class, educated patients have better access due to their ability to use voice to negotiate better services, and better health literacy to seek appropriate care. Choice has the potential to promote equity and contribute to reducing health inequalities if it is developed and implemented with the most disadvantaged in mind. Choice should also be developed in primary care and in care for people with long-term conditions, where choice has greater potential to empower patients, improve outcomes and reduce inequalities.

This report sets out a framework for progressive choice to ensure that disadvantaged patients are included and supported in choice policies. The framework also links choice to wider policies to engage people in their health and contribute to tackling health inequalities.

This framework has five themes:

- Building choice throughout the healthcare system, so that patients can be meaningfully involved in decisions about providers, treatments and services.

- Improving information, support and transport, empowering disadvantaged groups to make healthcare and health choices.

- Harnessing patient groups and other community and voluntary organisations to support disadvantaged groups and amplify their 'voice' to influence healthcare commissioners and providers.

- Developing choice in primary care so that more specialised services are available, tailored to needs, so that more care can be delivered outside hospital.

- Providing choice throughout care pathways relating to long-term conditions, empowering all patients to self manage their health.

Patient choice has many meanings and the debate has become confused. Choice emerged from rights movements that challenged paternalism and emphasised citizen empowerment. The rise of consumerism and the introduction of markets have created additional drivers for choice, based on creating contestability between providers to respond to individual preferences. We argue that, whilst consumerism and markets have roles as tools for improvement, the aim of choice should be to empower patients, improve outcomes and contribute to reducing inequity.

There are deep inequalities in health in England, compounded by inequities in access to healthcare in the NHS, including primary care. Our progressive vision for patient choice emphasises the potential benefits for disadvantaged groups by empowering patients and ensuring that the NHS meets their needs. Choice should be developed with goals of empowerment and improved outcomes wider than just focusing on markets.

Equitable access to choice – and equitable access to healthcare – matter for moral reasons. Equity is also key to ensuring that the extra resources in health prove effective. Sustained inequalities in health threaten the achievement of Wanless's scenario of full engagement of the public in their health (Wanless, 2002), and will end up increasing costs. However, our vision of progressive and equitable choices would contribute to tackling inequalities and engaging people in their health, by providing them with information and support on wider choices and in self-care.

Equity and choosing

Patients in the NHS are currently unequally involved in making decisions about their health and healthcare. This is due to a range of factors, including health literacy, language, education, disabilities, and digital exclusion. These inequalities are likely to become even more important to health as choice policy develops.

Choice has been piloted in several areas and specialties. The London project had positive equity findings, with disadvantaged groups participating in choice as much as other groups. However, the pilots have limited applicability to the choice policies that are being rolled out, and choice at referral has not been evaluated for equity. Whilst choice pilots have successfully delivered more equitable 'choosability' using Patient Care Advisers (PCAs) and support for transport as well as incentives for providers, these lessons have not been implemented in the roll-out of choice, when PCAs and support for transport will not be available nationally.

- Patients need to have access to accurate, relevant information in order to make choices. This information needs to be accessible, and measure health-related quality of life outcomes and wider factors of patient experience so that patients can make choices based on their particular needs and preferences.

- Independent sector providers should be subject to the same information requirements as NHS providers so that patients can have comparable information in order to make choices.

- Disadvantaged groups in particular require support and advocacy to make decisions and participate in choice. Support and advocacy should be commissioned from a range of sources, particularly from voluntary and community organisations that have good relationships with disadvantaged groups.

- Patients should be able to choose their source of information and support, and GPs could provide 'support prescriptions' for patients who might need targeted advice or advocacy.

- The provision of advice should be commissioned and regulated to ensure that high standards are maintained and disadvantaged groups are included. Primary care trusts (PCTs) will need to balance their spending priorities so that enough resources are available to commission effective information support and advocacy.

People without access to a car, who are often poorer and with greater health needs, are currently disadvantaged in access to the NHS. Choice could reduce the effects of transport inequality if patients can choose a time and place to suit them, particularly if they can choose care outside hospital. However, choice pilots showed that transport could act as a barrier to accessing choice.

- Provision of transport, assistance with organising transport or subsidy of the cost should be introduced so that less mobile people are not excluded from choice.

Equity, contestability and voice

Choice has been introduced in order to create contestability between providers, with the aim of improving quality and responsiveness. This has potential risks for equity, particularly if competition leads to polarisation, for example through service closures leaving areas under-served.

- Market management by commissioners and effective regulation must ensure that the operation of this market does not reduce choice, and does not create sink services for patients who are less able to move.

- Market entry and exit should be managed and regulated according to principles to protect equity and ensure fair competition.

- Providers that are losing patients need to be supported where necessary to ensure that essential services are maintained and that they can improve their services to meet patients' needs and preferences.

- Voluntary and community organisations that are providing information, support and advice for disadvantaged groups should gather intelligence on people's reasons for choosing, and on their experiences of providers. This information should be fed back to providers and commissioners so that services reflect patient requirements.

- Providers and commissioners will need to engage with communities more effectively to ensure their needs and preferences are being met.

Voluntary and community organisations, as well as good quality market research, will therefore provide information which ensures services respond to patients' voices, particularly the most disadvantaged.

This progressive vision would create a more patient-led NHS, with powerful collective voice backed up by the financial force of choice and Payment by Results.

Choice in primary care

At present government policy has concentrated on developing choice in secondary care. This could challenge the aim of shifting care from secondary to primary and preventative care.

It is not presently clear what choice means in primary care. From an equity point-of-view, lack of access to primary care can create barriers for patients, particularly those living in areas with closed GP lists or with GPs whose opening hours are difficult for people with unstable work or caring commitments. Patient transport is not provided for access to primary care. Quality of primary care can also be variable, and disadvantaged patients do not receive equitable treatments or referrals according to need.

- Greater choice of GP should be introduced. People with commitments that take them outside their home area should be allowed to register at a secondary practice near their place of work, or near to relatives. However, a greater benefit from increasing choice of GP would be to encourage more specialisation, either by a particular health need or demographic group.

- This vision of primary care could also improve the range of services available outside hospital, with networks of commissioning practices collaborating to provide a wider range of traditionally secondary services in the community.

Many of the mechanisms already exist to facilitate this transition. However, the current system for funding GPs is a barrier. At present most GPs are paid a salary or are funded according to historical patterns, rather than on the basis of the health needs of their population.

- A review of GP funding should look more broadly at paying GPs according to the needs of the patients they serve.

- There needs to be an 'Information revolution' in primary care to match the government's aim to increase information for choice in secondary care. Information needs to be backed up with support and advocacy for disadvantaged groups.

- Voluntary and community organisations should be commissioned to provide information and support and feed back to primary care the needs and preferences of local people.

People with long-term conditions would be the group most able to benefit from our vision of progressive choice based on empowerment and improving health. However, the current emphasis on choice of hospital does not serve this group's needs.

- Choice in long-term conditions needs to be developed throughout the pathway of care.

- A wider range of more specialist commissioners and providers in primary care would improve services for people with long term conditions, including choice of pathway and choice of disease or case management organisation.

- Choice could enable and incentivise patients to do more self management.

- As well as individual choice, the NHS, in partnership with voluntary and community organisations, should facilitate communities of patients who could support each other and participate in collective choices, strengthening the voice of disadvantaged groups and reversing historic inequities in the NHS.

The government has devoted significant resources to extending capacity and infrastructure to enable choice in secondary care. In order to ensure that choice works for disadvantaged gropus, the government will have to commit the necessary resources in information, support and advocacy. Extending choice in primary care, and for people with long-term conditions, will also require increased capacity to ensure that choices are available and that everyone will benefit.

Conclusion

Patient choice has the potential to reduce healthcare inequities and con-tribute to engagement of the public in their health. However, current choice policies risk increasing healthcare inequities and the wider potential benefits of patient empowerment will not be realised. This report sets out a vision for equitable, progressive choice in healthcare, providing patients with meaningful involvement, well supported in the community to ensure that disadvantaged groups are included.

The government needs to develop equitable choice policies in primary care as well as secondary care, and for the disadvantaged and those with long-term conditions as well as for the middle classes.

Acknowledgements

We would like to thank the project funder, Pfizer Ltd, without whose gener-osity we would not be able to conduct independent research.

We would like to thank everyone who presented, responded and par-ticipated at the policy seminars for this project, including Carol Propper, Michael Dixon, Elizabeth Manero, David Colin-Thomé and Steve Dunn. We would also like to thank all the people from the health policy and deliv-ery establishment, the research community, professionals and representa-tive bodies, and patient and community organisations who have helped us with research and discussions.

Thank you to Health Link for conducting the consultation with patient and community organisations in partnership with ippr, and to all the organisations that took part in the consultation. These were, Alzheimer's Society, ATD 4th World, Broadway, Council for Ethnic Minority Voluntary Organisations (CEMVO), FaithRegen, Mencap and Sign.

Our external readers, Anna Coote and Deborah Roche, provided invalu-able comments on the draft report for which we are grateful. We would also like to thank ippr colleagues including Peter Robinson and Howard Reed for their project direction and comments on the drafts; Nick Pearce, Jennifer Rankin, John Cannings and John Schwartz for their advice and assistance; and Deborah Roche (again) and intern Angus Steele for their early work setting the project up and conducting a literature review.

Introduction

Progressive vision of patient choice

Choice is at the heart of the government's public service reform agenda. In healthcare, patients will be offered new choices, in particular choosing between five hospitals for elective surgery by December 2005, and from any provider by 2008. Choices will also increasingly be developed in care outside hospital. Government ministers argue that this will reduce inequities in healthcare by providing choices to all, where before only the wealthy and articulate had been able to choose. Critics claim that choice will only benefit the middle classes, who have access to information and mobility, and that choice will lead to a two-tier health service, where left-behind patients receive poorer quality of care. This report argues for a progressive vision of choice in healthcare, where disadvantaged patients are empowered to make choices throughout their care to reduce healthcare inequities and tackle health inequalities. Choice should aim to do more than create a market. The primary goal of choice should be to improve outcomes and reduce inequalities.

The starting point for this project was to examine how choice – broadly defined – should be implemented to improve equity of access and reduce health inequalities. In moving the patient choice debate forward, this report recommends how choice can be developed and implemented in a more equitable way. It finds that choice is only likely to succeed in promoting equity and reducing health inequalities if it is sensitively developed and implemented with the most disadvantaged in mind and by drawing on the expertise and skills of voluntary and community-based groups.

The risks to equity are real. Choice could prove a costly misadventure if it is not specifically geared towards reducing inequity and improving health outcomes. If pro-equity policies are not implemented – particularly the provision of information and support to disadvantaged groups and ensuring that their preferences and experiences are acted on – then choice could increase inequalities. As well as being unjust, increasing inequity of access to health services would threaten the delivery of government health inequalities targets. Health inequalities currently represent a major barrier to the improvement of overall health outcomes, and thus the productivity of investment in health. Tackling health inequalities, including ensuring choice does not increase inequity, is therefore key to achieving the scenario of 'full engagement' set out by Wanless (2002).

Progressive choice also requires a significant expansion of the role and capacity of voluntary and community groups – such expansion would enhance their engagement in health services and ensure more proactive engagement in healthcare decisions. Disadvantaged groups would benefit more generally through the expansion of voluntary and community organisations that are particularly focused on supporting them.

The government has devoted a lot of resources to extending capacity to enable choice in secondary care. In order to ensure that choice works for the disadvantaged, the government will have to invest the necessary resources in information, support and advocacy. Extending choice in primary care, and for people with long-term conditions, will also require increased capacity to ensure that choices are available and that everyone will benefit.

Abandoning choice altogether would only sustain inequities and would not achieve engagement in health. If implemented equitably, the potential benefits of real patient choice are even greater.

Choice should be developed within a broader framework to tackle healthcare inequities and contribute to reducing health inequalities.

The framework for progressive choice includes the following themes:

- Building choice throughout the healthcare system, so that patients can be meaningfully involved in decisions about providers, treatments and services.

- Improving information, support and transport, empowering disadvantaged groups to make healthcare and health choices.

- Harnessing patient groups and other community and voluntary organisations to support disadvantaged groups and amplify their 'voice' to influence healthcare commissioners and providers.

- Developing choice in primary care so that more specialised services are available, tailored to needs, so that more care can be delivered outside hospital.

- Providing choice throughout care pathways relating to long-term conditions, empowering all patients to self manage their health.

Progressive choice would have wider social benefits than just off-setting inequities in choice. Real empowerment and engagement would improve concordance with treatment, improve health literacy and help people to make healthier choices in their lives. It would contribute to other aims that progressives value, such as social inclusion, nurturing social capital and improving public and user involvement in public services. Without these wider goals, patient choice will leave behind disadvantaged groups and an opportunity for transformation will be missed. Investment in progressive choice, would contribute to the transformation to 'full engagement' of the public in their health (Wanless, 2002) and a more equitable and sustainable health system.

Structure

Chapter one sets out the approach of the report. It discusses the background of choice in public services and healthcare, finding that the concept has become confused and dominated by the idea of creating a market. It discusses health inequalities and healthcare inequities, and sets out how some fear that patient choice could increase inequities.

Chapter two looks at how individuals might be disadvantaged by choice policies. It examines the premise that some groups will be better at 'choice' than others, focusing on how access and ability to use information to make choices, professional attitudes and behaviours, and practical barriers to accessing choices might disadvantage particular groups. It recommends how choice policies should be designed within a broader system of information and support, particularly focusing on the role of the voluntary and community sector. The chapter also explores practical assistance, including transport and regulation of geographical equity.

Chapter three examines the potential impact of quasi-markets in healthcare on equity. Whilst recognising the historic inequity of planned health systems, this chapter examines what impact contestability could have on geographic inequity, including the possibility of polarisation between succeeding and failing providers. It asks how choice might improve responsiveness and personalisation to individual needs, and sets out a framework for ensuring that disadvantaged groups' voices are heard.

Chapter four takes forward the lessons from this research to examine the options for developing patient choice in primary and community care, where the majority of healthcare takes place, and for the growing numbers of people with one or more long-term conditions.

Methodology

This report is based on research conducted by Joe Farrington-Douglas and Jessica Allen in spring and summer of 2005. The desk-based research by the researchers and an intern, Angus Steele, included literature reviews, grey literature searches and policy analysis. This was developed through a series of seminars, one-to-one meetings and ongoing communications with experts and stakeholders, including patient groups, professionals, academic experts and policy-makers. The researchers also attended debates and conferences. A mini consultation was held in partnership with Health Link, a public and patient involvement organisation, to explore with some voluntary and community organisations their potential to support our vision for equitable patient choice. We would like to thank all those we have met, who have presented at or attended seminars, or who have contributed by correspondence.

We would also like to thank the project funder, Pfizer, without whose support our work would not be possible.

1
Choice and equity

Choice policy

All parties have adopted the rhetoric of choice. However, the more it is used to justify policies and win votes, the less certainty there is for the public, front-line staff and policy-makers about what 'choice' really means. The background to choice in health and wider public services helps to explain the complex, sometimes conflicting, meanings of the current debate on public service reform.

The women's, anti-psychiatry and disability rights movements in the 1960s, 1970s and 1980s, brought the issue of 'choice' into health and social care services, particularly in the United States (Robinson, 2001). Family planning and anti-discrimination campaigners challenged the notion of professional autonomy and 'done-to' services, with excluded groups claiming choice over their fertility, and the choice to live independently. These developments foreran a broader patients' rights movement that challenged medical paternalism and asserted choice for patients over whether they took part in research or consented to risky treatment. Choice has therefore partly arisen from the idea of citizen empowerment.

However, the empowerment agenda has recently been supplanted by other developments. The information and communications technology revolution of the 1990s coincided with broader shifts associated with a more consumerist society. Informed, affluent citizens expect more choice in all areas of their life, leading to policy-makers demanding the same of public services. Research by ippr for the Wanless review (Wanless, 2002) found that people judge the NHS in relation to high street organisations that provide a range of services that are often tailored, responsive and flexible. There has also been a perceived shift in values, with voters less willing to elect explicitly tax-and-spend governments to pay for better public services, and more willing – if able – to 'opt out' and pay for private provision. It is in response to these perceived trends that political parties of all colours are using choice to win votes and justify often controversial public service reform policies.

Structural reforms have attempted to institutionalise choice to drive change and improvement. Purchasers and providers have been separated since the early 1990s, and choice at the point of referral from GP to hospital (known as 'choose and book') aims to create contestability between providers. In this new 'quasi-market,' patient choice is a way of allocating resources amongst providers to incentivise them to improve efficiency, quality and innovations by competing to attract patients. This approach is embodied by the system of Payment by Results (PbR), under which providers are paid at a set tariff for each treatment. Choice in public services is increasingly identified with the idea of a competitive market to motivate providers, with money following the user (be it patient, parent or passenger) rather than being allocated centrally.

These 'consumerist' and 'quasi-market' stories do not relay the whole background to choice in public services. If choice was just a concession to individualistic consumerism or a way of allocating resources, it would be difficult to argue for it in terms of progressive values. Despite the equitable founding principles of the NHS, financed through general taxation and free at the point of use according to need, analysis of usage according to need has shown that, proportionate to need, middle class people consume more NHS resources than people from poor backgrounds (Dixon et al, 2003).

Evidence suggests that there are some geographical inequities and unequal levels of mobility (for example related to car ownership) in access to services. More significantly, there are inequities due to different abilities to assert preferences and navigate the system. These inequities are compounded by unequal healthcare-seeking behaviours, which often disadvantage people from poorer, less educated backgrounds. Within the current 'planned' system there is 'choice and voice' for those who can negotiate successfully or who can pay to opt out, whilst there is less choice and voice and consequently poorer services and poorer health for disadvantaged groups. As this report explores, increasing patient choice could increase or decrease healthcare inequities due to unequal ability to choose, or 'choosability', depending on how choice policies are implemented.

In healthcare there are strong reasons for patient empowerment, including 'co-production' (for example improved concordance with treatments and self-management of chronic disease), improving quality of services, and enhancing active citizenship (Coulter, 2002). There is evidence that a sense of control from involvement in decision-making can improve health directly (Segal, 1998; Dixon, 2004). The process of patient involvement in healthcare and health can improve health literacy and help people to make healthier choices about their lifestyle and public health (Farrell, 2004).

The Wanless Report into the future funding of the NHS estimated that the added cost of not engaging the public in their health over the coming decades could be £30 billion per year by 2022/23 (Wanless, 2002). In particular, more self-care by patients was identified as a key area for improving productivity in the health system. From a progressive perspective, patient involvement in decision-making can improve people's feelings of control over their own lives and thus contribute to tackling social exclusion. 'Choice' as user empowerment is closely linked to ideas of public engagement, health improvement and self-determination.

Whilst current choice policies sometimes emphasise improving responsiveness and personalisation, driving quality and efficiency and equalising opportunities, choice can also be seen as a Trojan horse to achieve other aims. The 2005 Conservative election manifesto proposed patients' passports, where NHS patients could opt to 'go private' with a subsidy from the government. Framed in the language of choice was a policy that aimed to encourage more affluent middle classes to leave the NHS, institutionalising an unequal funding system where people with higher incomes could pay to receive a higher quality or faster service. So 'choice' can mean, for Conservatives, the choice to spend your money (if you have it) in a free market.

Choice is also associated with privatisation of the provision of public services. The development of choice, particularly with the emphasis on creating quasi-markets, has driven the policy of encouraging different providers. In order to generate 'contestability' (ie an element of competition between providers), the government has encouraged a range of providers from which purchasers, including patients, can choose. Whilst the majority of the increase in capacity in secondary care (hospitals and diagnostic and treatment centres) has been within the NHS, the government has agreed contracts centrally with multinational consortia to build and run diagnostic and treatment centres. The government has also encouraged – and at times compelled – purchasers to buy services from the independent and voluntary sectors. However, this policy is an optional route for enabling choice, rather than a necessity. Private provision, additional to or substituting for public provision, could be encouraged without patient choice; likewise patient choice could be implemented without providing independent sector options. The focus of this report is not on the implications of increasing private provision in healthcare, but on the implications and options for patient choice and equity.

Establishing a market in healthcare to incentivise providers has so far been the main driver for introduction of choice in the NHS. The flagship policy of choose and book will provide patients with a choice of four or five providers at the point of referral by December 2005, and a choice of any regulated provider able to treat patients at the tariff price by 2008. Creating contestability – rather than patient empowerment and involvement – is attractive to policy-makers driven by the aim to improve efficiency and performance in the NHS to meet waiting targets. Most of the targets in the NHS Plan relate to increasing output and improving access, whilst equity of access and patient oriented services remain softer aspirations not assessed by performance indicators.

A number of attempts have been made to list all the different choice policies that have been or might possibly be developed (National Audit Office, 2004; Perri 6, 2003; Appleby et al, 2003; Thompson and Dixon, 2004). Forty-four per cent of the general public and six per cent of GPs have been reported as not knowing what choice means (NHS Confederation,

2003). The NHS Confederation has argued that the term 'choice' might not be the right one. Blandly offering 'choice' as a panacea for public service reform could otherwise reduce public trust in politicians and in the direction of the reform agenda.

Some interpretations of 'choice' in healthcare

Introducing a 'quasi-market,' with providers competing for patients and money following the patients' choices.

- Quasi-markets do not require patient choice. For example, fundholding GPs in the 1990s made choices on behalf of their patients, and commissioning PCTs and GPs make choices on behalf of patients about what services are on the 'menu'.

- Creating market incentives has been the main reason for introducing patient choice of hospital (Catton, 2005).

- Not all patient choice options mean creating contestability. Contestability may require increasing plurality of providers, one option being to bring in more independent and voluntary sector provision. In some areas contestability may be impractical, for example for highly specialist procedures or for patients with complex needs, where fewer providers could safely treat them. Accident and emergency services and secure accommodation might be other examples where contestability is less appropriate.

Making services personalised to individual users

- Patients could be offered more choices about what services they receive, as well as where and when. For example, patients could help design their own long-term condition care plan, managed with a key-worker. Patients could make practical choices, for example what and when to eat, the time of their appointment or the sex of their doctor. Some choices may be clinical, others may be practical; personalisation might aim to meet individual needs or preferences. In a person-centred model, convenience and preference may be as equally important as clinical decisions.

- Choice of provider, especially when there is a limited range of options for more complex procedures, may on its own not deliver personalisation. Personalisation may be less efficient than standardised services, and there is always a limit to the capacity to meet every individuals' preferences.

Empowering users

- Professionals have traditionally made clinical decisions about patient care and protected their autonomy through self-regulation and ownership of knowledge. Patients have been encouraged to obey doctors' orders but this has contributed to disengagement and poor health decisions, especially for poorer, less educated or disadvantaged groups. Patient choice could counter medical paternalism and encourage equal participation in decision-making.

- Choice of time and location of hospital appointments on their own would probably not deliver change in patient–professional relationships. GPs can still direct patients and control the treatment options that they offer. Patient empowerment cannot happen unless professionals are engaged.

Enabling and encouraging co-production

■ Engaging patients to take part in the decisions about their healthcare could improve awareness of their condition and their capacity to self-care to improve outcomes and make more effective use of public services. Better communication is required to involve patients in making choices, which could improve concordance, improve outcomes of consultations and ensure needs of more disadvantaged groups can be met, as well as reduce medical error. Choice and patient involvement could help improve health literacy and reduce health inequalities.

■ Again, merely choosing between secondary care providers may be only a start and would not automatically improve co-production, patient involvement and health literacy.

Health equalities and healthcare equity

The focus of this report is on how choice can be delivered equitably and can contribute to reducing health inequalities. As an Institute founded on the idea of social justice, ippr is particularly concerned with the impact of the health system on health inequalities, and sees reducing inequalities between socio-economic, ethnic, geographic and other excluded groups as a primary aim of health policy. Whilst this report does not focus on the definitions and wider causes of inequity, some background on the challenges posed by health and healthcare inequality is relevant.

Successive independent inquiries have established the degree of inequality in health in the UK, and explored the determinants and policy implications (Black, 1980; Acheson, 1998). In 2002 the government set itself Public Service Agreement targets to reduce health inequalities between the areas with poorest health and the rest of society, measured in life expectancy; and between routine and manual socio-economic groups and the rest of society, measured in infant mortality. The targets aim for a 10 per cent reduction in inequalities by 2010, but most recently published data on health inequalities show that the targeted inequalities remain acute and are rising. Policies in place to tackle poverty and health inequalities, and progress in tackling some headline indicators, provide some ground for optimism but the overall challenge of health inequality in the UK is one of the greatest facing the current government, particularly if it is to deliver greater social justice (DH, 2005a).

Examples of health inequality (England and Wales)

Life expectancy at birth, 2001–03

	Highest local authority	Lowest local authority	Health inequality (relative)
Males	80.1 years – East Dorset	71.8 – Manchester	8.3 years (9.0%)
Females	84.8 – Kensington & Chelsea	77.6 – Blackburn & Darwen	7.2 years (9.2%)

Infant deaths per 1,000 live births, 2001–03, by socio-economic classification

Large employers and higher managerial	Routine	Sole registration of birth (sole parent)	'Other' (including workless)	Health inequality (relative)
2.9	6.6	7.4	8.9	7 deaths (306%)

Source: DH (2005a)

The data in the box above illustrate the degree of inequality in health suffered in Britain and the scale of the challenge for a government committed to social justice. The determinants of health are strongly linked to socio-economic background and geographical area. Whilst these inequities are evident across the social spectrum, our particular interest is the most disadvantaged groups. This is because groups facing multiple deprivations are more likely to experience social exclusion, contributing to child poverty and reduced life chances. Policies that address the needs of the most disadvantaged groups are also likely to help those higher up the social scale, yet they provide the biggest challenge for government and policy-makers.

To tackle health inequalities, the aim of the government should be two-fold – to reduce the actual inequalities in society through social policies such as employment initiatives, tackling poverty and raising the life chances of children from poorer backgrounds. The government also needs to address the links between social inequality and health inequality, including physical and social environments, psychosocial risk factors like stress, social networks and work stability, unhealthy behaviours and lack of healthcare-seeking and poor access to healthcare. The government's *Programme for Action* (DH, 2003a) identified four themes for the strategy to tackle health inequalities:

■ Supporting families, mothers and children.

■ Engaging communities and individuals.

■ Preventing illness and providing effective treatment and care.

■ Addressing the underlying determinants of health.

Many of these policies lie outside the field of healthcare, and success relies on cross-government commitments to reducing health inequality through social policies and other public services such as education and transport. Many of the causes of ill health are linked to inequality in society. Targeting services and public health interventions, as set out in the *Programme for Action*, will contribute towards reducing health inequalities. However it is not clear how much these interventions cost or how effective they are, making it difficult to prioritise or judge how best to invest (Wanless, 2004). The degree of socio-economic inequality in societies and communities is in itself a strong determinant of overall health outcomes (Wilkinson, 2005). Therefore, only by reducing inequality in society will greater health equality – and social justice – be delivered.

Whilst reducing health inequalities will not be delivered by healthcare alone, inequalities have been compounded by a health system that is also inequitable. Despite the fact that communities in poorer areas and people from deprived backgrounds have worse health, the provision of resources and the use of healthcare in poorer areas and by poorer groups remains inequitable, with lower access according to need than for wealthier and healthier groups. The 'inverse care law,' identified in 1971, suggested that areas that are poorer and have higher health needs are less well served than wealthier and healthier areas (Hart, 1971). This still remains a challenge for the NHS.

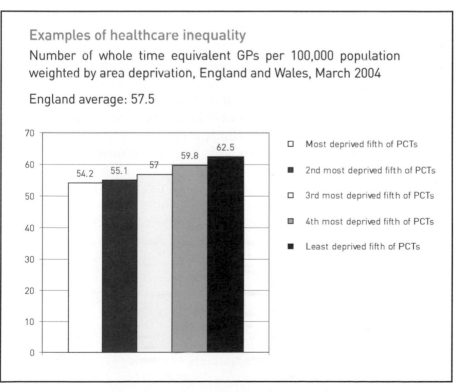

Examples of healthcare inequality

Number of whole time equivalent GPs per 100,000 population weighted by area deprivation, England and Wales, March 2004

England average: 57.5

Legend:
- Most deprived fifth of PCTs
- 2nd most deprived fifth of PCTs
- 3rd most deprived fifth of PCTs
- 4th most deprived fifth of PCTs
- Least deprived fifth of PCTs

Values: 54.2, 55.1, 57, 59.8, 62.5

Equity in healthcare is normally defined as equal access to healthcare to individuals in equal need. Importantly, this means responding differentially to individuals, taking into account their social and cultural situation and preferences as well as personal medical needs.

Dixon et al (2003) reviewed studies of access and use of primary and secondary healthcare in the NHS and concluded that inequities in healthcare still exist, particularly in relation to planned admissions and preventative care.

Examples of healthcare inequity

- Social classes IV and V had 10 per cent fewer preventative consultations than social classes I and II

- A one-point move down a seven-point deprivation scale resulted in GPs spending 3.4 per cent less time with the individual concerned

- Hip replacements were 20 per cent lower among lower socio economic groups, despite roughly a 30 per cent higher need

- Intervention rates of cardio angioplasty bypass graft or angiography following heart attack were 30 per cent lower in the lowest socio economic group than the highest

Dixon et al, 2003

The researchers tried to explain some of the causes of inequity in the NHS. These explanations and those found by Sihota and Lennard more recently are summarised in the box.

Sources of disadvantage in the NHS

- Distance and transport – transport (including access to a car) is more significant than distance

- Employment and personal commitments

- 'Voice', including knowledge of the system and ability to communicate with professionals

- Health beliefs and health seeking behaviour, including ability to identify symptoms.

Dixon et al, 2003

Health literacy and inequity

More recent research on 'health literacy' has identified links between health and healthcare use and education and social background. This is due to an 'inverse information law' whereby people in the greatest need of information about health are least likely to have access to it. Barriers to shared decision-making compound existing inequalities.

Sihota and Lennard, 2004

Although healthcare utilisation is only one factor in inequalities in health, the wider determinants of healthcare inequity are closely associated with the wider causes of health inequalities. Car ownership is negatively associated with deprivation, and people in less stable employment or with caring responsibilities are more likely to come from lower socio-economic and disadvantaged groups. Levels of education, literacy and communication skills are also associated with social factors which partly determine health and use of healthcare. What is harder to assess is how the health system should be changing to respond to these linked challenges of health and healthcare inequity so that it can meet the needs of disadvantaged individuals and contribute to reducing health inequalities.

Choice and equity

This report examines the real and potential implications of patient choice on equity of healthcare and health equality. Discussion about the impact of choice on equity is often polarised, with arguments that choice should be introduced to improve equity opposed by arguments that choice itself is a threat to equity. One proponent of choice in public services has observed that choice can be both justified and criticised on the same grounds of meeting demand, quality, efficiency and equity (Le Grand, 2004). This is in part a reflection of different interpretations of 'choice' and 'equity'. It also reflects the uncertainty about the actual policies that are being proposed, and the impact they might have on equity.

Choice and equity – summary of arguments in favour

Professional and administrative decision-making has not achieved equity. Wealthier patients can buy their way out of waiting lists, and assertive middle class patients can negotiate better services for themselves by using their voice within the NHS. By providing choice in healthcare you open up to everyone the choices currently only available to the 'posh and pushy'.

By allowing patients to express their preferences by taking their custom elsewhere, providers will be incentivised to respond to individual patients' needs, and will drive up quality in those hospitals that are currently providing poor quality services.

See, for example, Stevens, 2003; Reid, 2003

> **Choice and equity – summary of arguments against**
>
> Making choices can be more difficult for some people than for others. If ability to choose – 'individual choosability' – is unequally distributed, those who are better at making choices could choose better services and achieve better outcomes. If these skilful choosers are the educated middle classes who already have health advantages through the determinants of health and the ability to use voice within the NHS or to buy private healthcare outside the NHS, then choice could increase inequity and health inequalities. Wealthier patients will still be able to buy healthcare privately even if there is more choice in the NHS.
>
> A market in healthcare, moreover, with money following patients' choices, could create a two-tier system with high quality, responsive services for the wealthy and assertive, and 'sink' services for those less able to choose due to lack of information and skills, or because of practical barriers such as mobility and commitments. A planned system, with professional decision-making and fair rationing of resources to maximise population welfare rather than under-informed individual preferences, represents a surer route to equity of healthcare according to need.
>
> See, for example, Klein, 2003; Appleby et al, 2003

A progressive vision for equitable choices

Choice may lead to desirable ends, including improved efficiency through contestability and better allocation according to need, or improved average outcomes. However if, as we anticipate, choice increases inequity and fails to contribute to tackling health inequalities, this is unacceptable for a government committed to social justice and for a health service aiming to improve the health of the whole population. The key to ensuring that patient choice is delivered equitably lies in the design of the policy and its implementation. This report sets out a vision, backed up by practical recommendations, of how choice should be implemented to ensure that it does not increase inequity. We go further, setting out how choice could be supported in order to contribute to reducing healthcare inequities and tackling health inequalities.

A progressive vision of patient choice recognises and supports the potential for choice to contribute to a new citizenship. Taking responsibility for choices in healthcare is part of the process of citizenship. Whilst Barnes and Prior (1995) and Schwartz (2004) argue that exhortations to choose may be disempowering, we argue that responsibilities like participation in decision-making are intrinsic to citizenship. People who are engaged in their individual healthcare choices are more likely to take responsibility for their health and engage in collective decisions than patients who are told what services they will receive and where and how they will receive them.

By changing the relationship between the public and the service provider, 'choice' could encourage respect and responsibility for decision-making in public services. Choice policies should be linked with strategies to increase the capacity of the voluntary and community sector to support patients in decision-making and in making healthy choices. This could provide a collective forum for individual choice and for public engagement in decision-making, as well as developing healthy social capital and communities providing mutual support (Barber and Gordon-Dseagu, 2003). Patient choice should improve people's awareness of their rights and responsibilities, and can be implemented to help people to self-care, and to understand and make better choices in their daily life. In this way equitable choices could contribute to delivering the 'full engagement' scenario set out by Wanless (2002) in which investment in health leads to better outcomes for the whole population.

Equitable choices in public services require substantial investment, as none of the design solutions are cheap (Perri 6, 2003), and the government's estimation of the efficiency savings and costs of implementing choice information and support may be over-optimistic (Which?, 2005).

The economic case for equitable choices

ippr is concerned about health inequalities for social justice reasons. The fact that socio-economic inequality leads to ill health and premature death is unjust and immoral. Having rightly decided to increase patient-centredness and choice in the health service, the government has a duty to invest in the framework to ensure that choice does not increase inequity.

There is also a strong economic case for tackling health inequalities, and for implementing our vision of equitable, progressive choice. As Wanless highlighted in his reports for the Treasury, improving health outcomes for those with the worst health will be one of the important challenges for securing good health for whole population. If inequities in access to services – and inequalities in health – are not tackled as a matter of priority, then investment in health services will deliver less value for money. Inequitable access to services – in particular in preventative services – is one barrier to achieving the goals of reducing health inequalities in order to maximise the productivity of the health system (Wanless, 2004). Our vision for progressive and equitable choices would contribute to tackling inequalities and engaging people in their health, by providing them with information and support on wider choices and in self-care.

Conclusion

Patient choice has diverse meanings and the debate has become confused. Choice emerged initially from rights movements that challenged paternalism and emphasised citizen empowerment. The rise of consumerism and the introduction of markets have created additional drivers for choice based on creating contestability between providers to respond to individual preferences.

There are deep inequalities in health in England, compounded by inequities in access to healthcare in the NHS. Our progressive vision for patient choice emphasises the potential benefits for disadvantaged groups by empowering patients and ensuring that the NHS meets their needs. The benefits of implementing progressive choice would be felt throughout society, as not doing so would not only widen health inequalities but also increase healthcare costs. Choice should therefore be developed with wider goals than just creating a market.

The framework for progressive choice includes the following themes:

- Building choice throughout the healthcare system, so that patients can be meaningfully involved in decisions about providers, treatments and services.

- Improving information, support and transport, empowering disadvantaged groups to make healthcare and health choices.

- Harnessing patient groups and other community and voluntary organisations to support disadvantaged groups and amplify their 'voice' to influence healthcare commissioners and providers.

- Developing choice in primary care so that more specialised services are available, tailored to needs, so that more care can be delivered outside hospital.

- Providing choice throughout care pathways relating to long-term conditions, empowering all patients to self manage their health.

Equitable access to choice – and equitable access to healthcare – matter for moral reasons. Equity is also key to ensuring that the extra resources in health prove effective. Sustained inequalities in health threaten the achievement of Wanless's scenario of full engagement of the public in their health, and will end up increasing costs. However, our vision of progressive and equitable choices would contribute to tackling inequalities and engaging people in their health, by providing them with information and support on wider choices and in self-care.

2
Equity and choosing

Patient involvement in decision-making

This chapter addresses how patient choice should be developed and implemented in ways that improve equity. We explore how capacity to make choices and access best services should be available for everyone, particularly those from disadvantaged groups. Based on our research, discussions and consultation with voluntary and community organisations, we draw lessons from current choice policy that should apply as choice is rolled out into primary care.

At present choice is likely to be used by middle class patients to negotiate more and better services, potentially reinforcing existing health inequalities. It is therefore critical to ensure that choice is made more equitable and policymakers and professionals maximise patient involvement in decision-making.

However, professionals often have different ideas about the extent to which patients should be, and are, involved in decisions. Professionals may underestimate the appetite and potential for patient involvement in decision-making, and may interpret choice as an opportunity to manage and control patients' behaviour rather than engaging them as partners in decision-making (Farrell, 2004). An international study found the UK health system was the worst among six countries at involving patients in choices and advising patients on healthy choices (Schoen et al, 2004). Patient satisfaction and real trust depend on autonomy and involvement in decision-making (Mechanic, 1998).

The evaluation of the choice pilot in London found that less than a third of patients eligible for the scheme were offered a choice by their consultant (Coulter et al, 2005). International experience suggests that, although patient choice of hospital may be officially provided, in practice the referring doctor's voice may be stronger than the patient's (Thomson and Dixon, 2004). Despite professional codes of practice and training that emphasise patient autonomy and communication skills (for example, the General Medical Council's code of practice), the Healthcare Commission's State of Healthcare 2005 report concluded that 'there is worrying evidence on how [patients] receive information, what information they receive, and whether they are involved in decisions about their care' (Healthcare Commission, 2005).

Involving patients in decision-making must be well-supported. Experiences with choice pilots suggest that information, support and practical assistance can help people to make decisions about where they would like to be treated. For example, patients in Greater Manchester were more likely to take up choice if they discussed their needs with a Patient Care Adviser (PCA) (Barber et al, 2004) and in London patients who did not take up the offer of a choice were less likely to be satisfied with the information they received (Coulter et al, 2005).

Improving health literacy, self-care and reducing health inequalities depend on developing new patient–professional relationships (Coulter, 2002; Byng et al, 2003; Sihota and Lennard, 2004). Whilst there might still be occasions where patients delegate decisions to professionals in emergencies or in particularly complex situations, the overall objective of choice policies should be to promote shared decision-making because, as we suggested in chapter one, this is inherently beneficial to patients.

Changes are being made to medical training to emphasise communication skills (Modernising Medical Careers, 2005). This welcome move needs to be expanded to engage all professionals, including support staff. Patient involvement should therefore be a stronger theme in clinical governance. All healthcare providers should be regulated to ensure that they are involving patients in decision-making and ensuring that people are not excluded from choice. The National Standards for Better Health, and individual professional standards, should reflect the importance of choice and patient involvement so that it is recognised as a core component of quality.

Choosing and equity

As discussed in chapter one, the NHS is inequitable at least partly because of inequities in ability to access better services. These inequities compound wider inequalities in society that affect health. There is therefore a considerable risk that extending choice in healthcare might benefit wealthy and educated middle class patients. Which? (2005) found that choice is likely to widen existing inequalities in health and access to healthcare, and Lent and Arend (2004) propose a gradualist approach to developing choice as capacity and experience grow. Professionals in particular believe that choice will increase inequity, with only 5 per cent of GPs believing that choice will reduce health inequalities (National Audit Office, 2005). This illustrates the gap between policy-makers and staff about the impact of current choice policy, as well as the lack of professional engagement in current choice policies.

Some surveys have indicated inequities in desire and ability to choose – what we call 'choosability'. A survey of London patients' willingness to consider an alternative hospital found significant correlations between patients' willingness to consider choosing and certain characteristics, including age (being under 60), educational status (educated beyond statutory school leaving age), household income (above average earnings) and health status (rated as 'good' by respondents) (Coulter et al, 2005). Similarly, research by

Which? (2005) found a low desire for patient choice of hospital in specific groups. People from higher socio-economic groups were more confident about demanding choice and understood the choices offered, compared with people from lower socio-economic groups, particularly those with poor English. The argument is frequently made that patients do not want choice of provider; they simply want a good local service (for example Hattersley and Pollock, quoted in Public Administration Select Committee, 2005).

The desire for choice – theory to reality
However, other research has reached different conclusions about the appetite for choice. A MORI (2003) survey for Birmingham and the Black Country Strategic Health Authority found that most respondents in the area welcomed the idea of choice of hospital, although many lacked confidence to do it on their own and wanted advice and information to help them decide. Middle-aged and lower socio-economic groups in this survey were more attracted to the idea of choosing a hospital than other age groups and higher socio-economic groups. However, older people and people from lower socio-economic groups were also more likely to prefer to delegate choice entirely to their GP. These findings at least indicate the difficulties in selective use of statistics in making generalisations about the socio-economic determinants of appetite and capacity to choose (for example in National Audit Office, 2004).

There is a difference between what people say in surveys about the idea of choice and how they act in practice. There have been more positive findings in the evaluations of choice pilots in London. Following its initial survey work, the Picker Institute audited the take-up of the offer of choice at six months (where patients waiting longer than the target were given the choice of a shorter wait at an alternative provider in London). Two-thirds of patients offered a choice moved to a different provider with a shorter waiting time, and most of the differences between socio-economic groups in willingness to choose had disappeared (Coulter et al, 2005). The progressive argument for patient choice aims to equalise 'choosability' to bring benefits for disadvantaged groups – to provide a level playing field for patients, ensuring that everybody can access the best services to meet their needs and have more control over decision-making.

What we can learn from choice pilots?
The wider value of the findings of the English choice pilots such as the London Patient Choice Project (LPCP) should be qualified. The LPCP's aim was to manage the waiting lists of a geographic area using choice to allocate waiters more evenly (Dawson et al, 2005). Critically, patients were provided with the option of free transport and choice was supported by

significant investment in capacity and infrastructure. Specially-employed PCAs were appointed to support patients in decision-making. Two-thirds of eligible patients were not offered choice for various reasons, and choice was restricted to people who had been waiting for operations for more than six months.

The government's policy of patient choice at the point of referral aims to create a quasi-market where money follows the patient, incentivising providers to improve efficiency and quality. This is a significantly different proposition to choice at six months. Where choice at the point of referral was tested, the impact on equity was not studied (Taylor et al, 2004). As waiting times diminish to 18 weeks from referral to treatment, so will the significance of waiting on a patient's decision to choose a hospital, and other factors such as distance, reputation, convenience and quality will play a greater role. This means that the lessons from the choice pilots might be difficult to transfer.

In the national roll-out of patient choice, the funding and support provided in the pilots, including PCAs and transport, will not be available. Therefore the positive equity findings from the pilots should not be expected. Choice is likely to increase inequity. As a first step, therefore, the government and the NHS should ensure that there is high quality evaluation of the impact of choice on equity, both in terms of access to choice and to services. This would provide an evidence base from which lessons from policy experiments can be continuously learned. Support for choice should be targeted towards groups that are identified as being disadvantaged.

Equitable choice information and health literacy

In order to implement choice equitably, decisions should be well informed. The need for easy to access good quality information is particularly acute as the importance of waiting times in affecting choice diminishes. The government has acknowledged the need for an 'information revolution' in the NHS to facilitate choice at referral – and we are likely to see a market in information provision open up. Equally, if not more important, is that patients, particularly those from disadvantaged backgrounds who may already have poor health literacy, are supported to access, understand and use the information to make the right choices for them. There will need to be PCAs and much more involvement of community and voluntary organisations to support patients. Disadvantaged patients will also need practical support to access their choice of provider so that inequality in mobility is not an additional barrier.

In choice pilots the level of information provided was fairly basic – waiting times, star ratings and some indicators of performance based on national targets. Even though the pilots of six-month choices were essentially based on waiting times, patients voiced a desire for more information on which to base their choices (Coulter et al, 2005).

Unmet information needs in London Patient Choice Project

- Safety record

- Standards of hygiene

- Surgeon's qualifications/experience

- Quality of patient care

- Operation success rates

- Arrangements for follow-up care

- Experience of treating this condition

Coulter et al, 2005

A MORI survey for the Department of Health found that 90 per cent of respondents wanted more information in order to make choices about their treatment or care (DH, 2003b). Organisations responding to the government's consultations on choice and equity expressed the importance of information so that people could make informed choices (Help the Aged, 2003; Long-term Medical Conditions Alliance, 2003), and the government's White Paper acknowledged that an 'information revolution' was needed (DH, 2003b).

'Star ratings are pretty meaningless for making choices. Patients need information that is more relevant to user experience, but it is important to distinguish clinical outcomes and patient experience data. Patients could place more importance on quality of aftercare or support with living with their condition post-operation, rather than just on consultants.'

ippr/Health Link interview with CEMVO

The provision of extra information and PCAs in the choice at six months pilots raised patients' satisfaction with information. More importantly, pilot studies in London and Manchester and for patients waiting for cardiac surgery have consistently shown that the provision and use of information is a key determinant of the take-up of choice (Coulter et al, 2005; Barber et al, 2004; Le Maistre et al, 2004).

Disadvantaged groups may have greater difficulties in accessing and using information due to literacy, language, cognitive or sensory impairment, mental illness or lack of access to information technology. A more equitable choice programme needs to identify the risks and barriers to informed decision-making and then mitigate them so that all groups and individuals have the opportunity to make informed choices.

Improving access to and use of information on healthcare and wider health knowledge would contribute towards health literacy and reducing healthcare inequities and health inequalities. Lack of information contributes to inequality in outcomes, including acting as a barrier to self-care (DH, 2005b; Corben and Rosen, 2005; Sihota and Lennard, 2004). The information for choice strategy must be integrated into a wider strategy involving patients more in the pre-referral decisions, including making healthy choices, treatment choices and choice in primary care. Chapter four recommends how choice should be extended into primary care and for people with long-term conditions.

What type of information do people need?

At present, the website www.nhs.uk provides information on prospective waiting times, access and patient experience and quality, taken from the Healthcare Commission's performance ratings. Evaluations of choice pilots found a significant and unmet need for better information on the quality of care by alternative providers (Le Maistre et al, 2004; Coulter et al, 2005; Taylor et al, 2004).

Publication of clinical quality information might also improve quality, as Hibbard et al (2003) found in a controlled trial in America. Publishing information on outcomes of surgical teams was recommended by the Bristol Inquiry (Bristol Royal Infirmary Inquiry, 2001) in order to improve patient safety and regulate quality. Patients have also expressed a desire to base their choices on information on expertise of the surgeon and operation success rate (MORI, 2005a).

There are risks associated with publishing individual surgeons' death rates without better risk-adjustment. Publication of surgical mortality figures is particularly controversial, possibly incentivising professionals to select less risky patients more likely to survive surgery (Treasure, 2005). However, the Freedom of Information Act in the UK has encouraged surgeons and hospitals to publish mortality rates (Bridgewater, 2005; The Guardian, 2005; St George's Healthcare NHS Trust, 2005). The ability of patients to use information to make rational choices is limited. Rational decision-making is rare, as poor information, understanding and emotional involvement create barriers to rationality – as in the MMR vaccine scare (Cowling, 2005). People may make poor decisions due to 'individual failures' such as technical inability, weakness of will or inexperience (New, 1999). However, professionals are also at risk of individual failure and may be less motivated to make the best decisions. Therefore these challenges should be addressed with better information and support, rather than be accepted as barriers to empowerment (Le Grand, 2003).

There is more to measuring quality of outcome than mortality statistics. For patients who survive surgery, other outcome measures should be used and published to inform patients' choices. Generic and condition-specific measures of health-related quality of life outcomes (HRQoL) should be measured at suitable follow-up periods to ascertain the medium and longer-term success of healthcare interventions (Appleby and Devlin, 2005). Some private healthcare providers have developed the practice internally using patient-assessed HRQoL measures, for example Short Form 36 (Vallance-Owen et al, 2005). These should be introduced on a sample basis in the NHS and published so that patients can choose providers based on comparison of outcomes other than mortality. Other usable and user-determined measures of quality of life should also be developed, to improve knowledge and ability to manage health (Long-term Medical Conditions Alliance, 2003). Better measurement of outcomes, including user-determined measures, is also useful to measure productivity and cost effectiveness of interventions.

Other types of information

Whilst there is demand from patients for information on quality, other information is also important for many people. Many patients know that providers must satisfy particular levels of quality and would prefer to make choices based on convenience and other preferences. One important goal of choice should be to provide more personalised services. Therefore provision of information on a wide range of issues, not just clinical, is important. Health Link (2000) conducted a study with disadvantaged groups in London to establish their choice information needs. This research uncovered a wide array of needs, which also reflected the unmet needs of disadvantaged groups (see box).

Information disadvantaged patients need when choosing a hospital

1. Facts on access

a. Transport, including getting to hospital by public transport, using hospital transport systems, driving to hospital

b. Access to treatment, including waiting times, and waiting times for each procedure if more than one

c. Disability Discrimination Act compliance, including hospital environments, processes and staff skills

2. Facts on quality

a. General performance information, including star ratings, patient survey results, mortality rates, cancellations, cleanliness, infection rates and doctor-to-patient ratios

b. Environment, including single sex wards, telephones, televisions and radios, ward size, confidentiality, prayer space, smoking areas, disabled access, canteen, provision of information, children's wards, facilities for adolescents, facilities for parents, education, facilities and equipment for disabled children, information for children

---

c. Staff, including skills in dementia, staff for children, staff training and skills including English speaking and cultural awareness, staff training and skills affecting children and parents

3. Ward and hospital processes

a. Ward processes, including occupational therapy, culturally appropriate food, feeding procedures and processes affecting children and parents, including food and accommodation.

b. Hospital-based processes, including visiting rules, follow-up care, communication systems

4. Hospital, staff attitudes or other subjective matters

a. Aspects of reputation, including for the particular treatment(s) and of the particular surgeon

b. Interaction with patients, including respect for privacy, quality of nursing, communication with patients

c. Other subjective issues, including team working, quality of food and follow-up care

Health Link, 2004

Innovative ways of presenting information which patients can use to inform their choices are being explored. Some would like to receive information from other patients. A website allowing patients to post their 'reviews' of healthcare providers has been set up by a social entrepreneur and GP in Sheffield (www. patientopinion.org). This builds on the popularity of online retailers such as Amazon.com that provide forums for customers to review products to inform other customers' choices. The likelihood is that patients will self-select, risking unrepresentative opinions being posted. However, it may be more reliable than patients basing decisions on media reports, anecdote and rumour. Websites should be developed using a representative sample of patients. Voluntary and Community Sector (VCS) organisations that have direct contact with health services users, for example older people's organisations or patient support groups such as Alzheimer's Society or cancer groups, should be supported to provide a reviewing service for other patients that could complement the centrally organised national patient survey programme.

ippr and Health Link conducted research to explore how community and voluntary sector organisations might provide information. Some organisations currently provide information relevant to the needs of their client group. For example, the homeless organisation Broadway provides information on hospitals where homeless people are treated with respect and Council of Ethnic Minority Voluntary Sector Organisations (CEMVO) signposts people to providers where minority languages are spoken.

Health Link is developing an information tool bringing together new and existing data to provide disadvantaged patients with information so that they can make informed choices about the best hospitals for them. Collecting and publishing this information could itself drive providers to improve their performance on patient-centred aspects of quality. Spreading this good practice, monitoring and providing local information needs, particularly of disadvantaged groups, will be central in ensuring the right information is available.

With greater use of a wider range of providers, patients need to be able to compare different options. Currently, performance information is only published for NHS providers. This includes, for example, results from staff and patient surveys in hospitals and primary care; clinical measures including death rates and emergency readmissions; MRSA infection rates; risk management standards; quality of food; and cleanliness of wards.

NHS-commissioned independent sector providers should be subject to the same provision of information obligations as the NHS. For patients to make choices – and to ensure fair regulation – these measures should also be published for independent and voluntary sector providers treating NHS patients. Private sector providers currently collect quality information to monitor performance internally, but this is not available to the public. Wherever NHS patients are treated by alternative providers under the patient choice policy, comparable information should be made available. The principle of informed choice, as well as public accountability and value for money, should override concerns about commercial confidentiality. Publication of quality information for choice and accountability should be a condition of market entry. As ippr has argued before, transparency in public–private partnerships would also increase quality and improve connection and trust between the user and the state (Maltby and Gosling, 2004).

Sources of information

Ensuring that all patients have access to information is vital in ensuring equity. Patients need to have options about how they access information so they can use the sources that best meet their needs. Particular care needs to be taken to ensure that disadvantaged groups are not further disadvantaged by an 'inverse information law' (a trend identified by Sihota and Lennard (2004) whereby those in greatest need of health information have the least access to it).

GP as source of information
In surveys, many patients say that they currently get information from their GP and would prefer their GP to be the main source (Coulter et al, 2005; MORI 2003; Taylor et al, 2004). Older people in particular value face-to-face discussions. This may in part reflect the professional monopoly of

health information. Patients have not traditionally been empowered to access and understand health information and there have not been many reliable alternatives to GPs.

Part of the objective of introducing choice and shared decision-making is to encourage a dialogue and greater sharing of information between doctor and patient. Where possible, GPs should provide information to patients as a matter of course, and choice should create an opportunity for this to happen in all consultations. Professional and quality regulation by the General Medical Council and the Healthcare Commission should recognise the importance of information provision and shared decision-making. The Quality and Outcomes Framework to reward GPs should also be adjusted to incentivise greater information and choice support.

'Although some GPs are better, not all clients get the referrals they need. People are told there is not much that primary care can do, GPs need to have better information to give patients – even if it is just referring them to the Alzheimer's Society for more information and support.'

ippr/Health Link interview with Alzheimer's Society branch

However, there is currently limited capacity for GPs to provide all the information to help patients make choices. About 50 per cent of patients would require extended consultations if GPs were to fulfil the information brokerage role (Barber et al, 2004) and GPs are concerned about the increased burden (National Audit Office, 2005). Practice-based commissioning may lead to a conflict of interest in GPs giving information about the services they are commissioning and perhaps also providing. Healthcare professionals often appear pressed for time, and do not provide opportunities for patients to ask questions (Sihota and Lennard, 2005). GPs have ongoing relationships with secondary care providers which could influence the way they present information to patients; this could increase with payment by results as secondary care income depends on the choices of patients at the point of referral.

The government has so far struggled to engage the medical profession in the choice and involvement agenda. Better engagement of professionals in the development of choice and public involvement is needed to ensure that a patient-led NHS can be delivered. GPs will have to be convinced that they are not being burdened with a raft of new responsibilities to provide information and support for choice. Whilst GPs should provide more information to patients – not just on hospital choices but on treatment and self-care options – their role might be more of a first point of contact, referring patients to other sources of information, including VCS organisations.

Other health and social care professionals will also be central in delivering equitable choices, providing information and support to disadvantaged patients, and involving patients in decision-making throughout their care pathway. Nurses, primary care professionals, allied health professionals, social workers and carers also need to be engaged and supported in helping patients choose. Specialist professionals, for example speech and language therapists or sensory impairment social workers, will play an important role in ensuring that particularly excluded groups can access and understand information (NHS Alliance, 2004; Byng et al, 2003).

Online and digital information

The website www.nhs.uk provides extensive information about performance ratings and practical information on location and transport. This is being developed to make it easier for patients to compare the options of different providers to facilitate the choose and book policy. Patients with access to the internet, either at home, work or in the community, will be able to view this information and make informed choices using secure passwords, or they can view the information and book it in the consultation room with their GP. The nhs.uk website provides a range of options for making it easier for people with sensory or motor impairments to access information, including larger text size, access keys and 'Browsealoud'. With these advantages, online information sources can often be more useful and more accessible to disadvantaged groups than leaflets, reports or time-pressed GPs.

> 'Homeless people like face to face explanations but easy to use, straightforward IT systems should be available to all people. Internet based information should be developed for the general public, so that clients can do their own research. It should be well signposted.'
>
> ippr/Health Link interview with Broadway, homeless organisation

However, online information provision will not meet the needs of the more disadvantaged members of the community. Internet access reflects social class, with 79 per cent of social grade AB compared with 33 per cent of social grade DE using the internet. Older people and disabled people have less access to the internet, despite higher needs (MORI, 2005b). Other new technologies such as digital TV also have the potential to help people access information and make choices and the NHS will use these to enable choose and book. However, these technologies also risk compounding healthcare inequalities (Sihota and Lennard, 2005) as use and access to them reflect wider inequalities.

> 'Clearly, lower socio-economic groups, disabled people and older
> people are at risk of exclusion from choose and book if it is exclusively
> dependent on web-based information and processes.'
>
> Health Link, 2004

ippr has recently argued that, as part of its wider technology and education policies, the government should ensure that technological advance is
used to extend social and economic benefits. This would include targeted
ICT training so that disadvantaged groups are not excluded from electronic
patient records or patient choice (Davies, 2005).

IT knowledge brokers should also be provided in the community, as
piloted in the Oxford Patient Access to their Online Electronic Health
Record (EHR) Project where information support workers introduced
patients to their online EHR (Pyper, 2002). GP practices should have
internet terminals available for patients to access a range of health information. Knowledge brokers could be available on some days to help
patients. Other public access IT knowledge brokers should be based in
libraries, Connexions and Sure Start centres and wider community locations; some librarians in London have been trained to help patients with
choose and book.

Patient Care Advisers

Alternative sources of information have been piloted. In the Manchester,
London and Cardio Heart Disease choice at six months projects, PCAs were
provided to broker information and guide patients through the system
from telephone call centres. PCAs were a popular innovation and helped
to ensure that more people got the information they wanted to choose an
alternative hospital. However, there was still inequality in the extent to
which PCAs met the information needs of all patients, with non-choosers
less satisfied with the information provided. Some patients found PCAs in
Greater Manchester confusing, more so amongst those who did not take up
the offer of choice (Barber et al, 2004).

However, for the national roll-out of choice in England, patient care
advisers will not be provided with centrally allocated resources (Public
Administration Select Committee, 2005). This is a deficiency in patient
choice policy that urgently needs to be rectified if choice is to be implemented equitably.

The Department of Health and the Prime Minister's Delivery Unit identified quality of information and PCA service as being important factors in
ensuring patients are able to take up choice. At present government intervention has been to provide good practice guidelines on providing information and PCAs (DH, 2005c). However, for choice in secondary care and as

choice is developed in primary care it is crucial that the government, regulators and the NHS ensure that adequate information support is resourced and provided, in even greater depth and breadth than was provided in the more limited choice at six months pilots.

One option that PCTs will consider is to develop the PCA function that was provided in the pilots. PCAs or information brokers will have to learn the lessons from the pilots to ensure that they are more accessible to disadvantaged patients. They will have to provide a broader information brokering role than in the six month pilots so that patients can choose on the basis of a range of quality information rather than just on waiting times. PCT commissioned information brokers should have to meet high service standards and be regulated by the Healthcare Commission.

National standards for information brokers

Information brokers should not be an add-on or marginal service but should be a core service priority. PCTs should be responsible for proving or commissioning information brokers to centrally set national standards, self-assessed and regulated by the Healthcare Commission to ensure that service users receive a guaranteed level of service. Information broker standards should include commitments to equity, ensuring that access to information is ensured for disadvantaged groups. National standards should include:

- Availability in different languages. PCAs in London and Manchester choice at six months pilots had access to Language Line interpreting facilities, but this was not available if service users had follow-up questions at a later date

- Adequate training in patient-centred communication skills

- Audited quality of information provided

- Provision of core information on quality of providers

- Provision of practical information on providers and navigation of the choice system

- Continued advice throughout the care pathway, including post-operative follow-up

- Provision of information and advice to all patients rather than only to those who want to choose

- Signposting users to sources of information and support in the community, including patient support groups and other voluntary and community groups

- Recording feedback from service users on the quality of services

- Equity audit to ensure all groups receive adequate information

Information brokers should be provided in GP practices to help people navigate the choices offered to then. Citizens' Advice currently provides information and advocacy in some hospitals and surgeries. PCTs and practices should commission organisations such as citizens advice bureaux (CABx) to provide high quality, trained and independent advice to help patients access information and make choices. Citizens Advice has recommended that local advice services (or in our terms information brokers) be rolled out in healthcare locations (Citizens Advice, 2004). They could also link people to expert patient programmes and condition or demographic specific support and advocacy groups. Citizens Advice is particularly suitable as an information broker as it has experience in dealing with disadvantaged groups, has excellent training programmes in information sharing for staff and typically has a wide knowledge base about support organisations.

Advice, support and advocacy

Health service users say that they want more information to make choices, and provision of information is important to spread the opportunity to choose. However, international evidence and evaluations of choice pilots suggest that information only has a small impact on decision-making for healthcare 'consumers', and less educated and older people can have lower information processing skills (Burgess et al, 2005; Hibbard et al, 2001). So information alone is insufficient to empower patients and create equitable patient choice.

Experts interviewed in our research agreed that support in making choices was as important as provision of information, particularly for potentially excluded groups which would be left behind if choice were provided. Lack of access to information and ineffective communication by healthcare professionals creates barriers to involvement in decision-making. If patient choice policies are rolled out without specific support for these and other disadvantaged groups then these groups could be increasingly disadvantaged.

VCS organisations should play a key role in supporting and advocating for disadvantaged groups to enable them to make informed choices and help them to meet their wider health and social needs. These groups are ideally placed as they already have contact with disadvantaged groups and an understanding of their needs and are experienced in offering support and advocacy. The Social Exclusion Unit's (SEU) interim report *Improving Services, Improving Lives* (2005) recognised the role that the VCS could play in ensuring that public services reach disadvantaged groups. In particular it recommended a role for the VCS in sharing expertise and acting as an intermediary, providing a voice for disadvantaged groups. There are already networks of patient organisations that could provide information and support for choice. These organisations should also be involved in facilitating peer networks to support patients to make decisions and self-care, particularly for long-term conditions (Corben and Rosen, 2005).

Community organisations could also play a part, for example older people's or minority ethnic organisations. There is a risk that not all disadvantaged groups would have access to such organisations, particularly where there is less civic activism in their community. Healthcare providers should therefore signpost patients to organisations that can support them, including Citizens' Advice or a relevant health-related organisation.

Involvement of the VCS also carries risks relating to the quality of information and advice provided. However, the government already uses the sector to provide some aspects of patient care, including supporting social care service users to make use of direct payments (DH, 2004a). A strategic agreement was published in 2004 between the Department of Health, the NHS and the VCS, setting out a framework to promote the increasing role of the VCS in contributing to health service planning and delivery (DH, 2004a). Any risk in involving the sector in supporting patients with choice could be managed by effective contract agreements with organisations that provide information, support and advocacy.

Two projects are currently underway in Birmingham and Manchester examining how voluntary sector organisations could provide information and support in patient choice. These will provide useful lessons for how patient choice could be made available for all. However, it will be important that, unlike the six months choice pilots, these lessons are implemented and funded.

Our research with VCS organisations confirms that there is a desire in the sector both to support disadvantaged patients in accessing information and making choices, and to contribute to public involvement in collective health decision-making. Rather than struggling to get their voices heard, organisations serving and representing disadvantaged groups should be engaged by the NHS.

Support prescriptions

The government announced in 2004 that it would explore the idea of 'information prescriptions', where professionals and patients could record discussions about diagnosis and treatment, and professionals could signpost people to sources of information and support relevant to their condition and circumstances (DH, 2004b). This idea should be implemented to accompany the roll-out of patient choice so that people can access tailored information to help them make choices about providers and treatment options. The government and the NHS should also develop 'support prescriptions' so that professionals can refer patients – particularly those from disadvantaged backgrounds – to independent support and advocacy workers in the VCS. This should be accompanied by funding that would follow the patient so that the VCS support workers can allocate sufficient resources to providing these important services. This would also help to signpost patients who are not already served by a voluntary organisation like an ethnic, faith, disability or health condition group.

'Choice in health is a massive challenge for this group. The implementation of choice should not be rushed, but thoroughly prepared and the process should be accessible to all patients. All the tools should be there, such as funded specialist health advocacy organisations, good information for the general public and for voluntary groups. We should be pleased to do the work, since choice is a positive development and we want to see our clients participate and be supported, possibly by having a full-time specialist worker.'

ippr/Health Link interview with Broadway, homeless organisation

'We have excellent links to hard to reach groups; they feel comfortable with us and trust us.'

ippr/Health Link interview with FaithRegen, minority ethnic and immigrant community organisation

Ethnic and language minorities

Patients from minority ethnic backgrounds have worse health outcomes than the rest of society (Acheson, 1998). One factor compounding health inequality is that, for those whose first language is not English, access to health services is curtailed by the extra barriers they face.

'Language barriers that inhibit individuals from using health services are another important inequality issue. The NHS survey of patients asked people whether or not there was anyone available to help with interpreting when visiting the GP or health centre. Forty-three per cent relied on a relative or friend, 16 per cent on someone from the surgery or health centre and 41 per cent said there was no one available to interpret for them.'

Coulthard et al, 2004

As more choice is offered in the NHS it will become increasingly important to ensure that information and communication is available in a range of languages. NHS Direct has made a framework agreement with a universal written and spoken translaton and interpreting service that NHS organisations can commission. This needs to be used by PCTs to help communication throughout the care pathway.

The specific choice needs of minority ethnic patients also need to be met. As choice is rolled out there will be greater need and scope for organisations like CEMVO and the VCS organisations it represents to ensure that potentially excluded minority ethnic patients have access to advice and advocacy, including translation and interpreting. Where the VCS is commissioned or accredited to provide information support and advocacy, it should have similar access to translation and interpretating as statutory services. For example, CancerBACUP provides a multilingual free phone helpline in 12 non-English languages, and Speakability's helpline has access to Language Line interpreters. This would help the government's policy of opening up provision of services and building the capacity of the VCS.

'New refugee groups have particular language and cultural needs that can be supported by the voluntary and community sector. We provide signposting for people from ethnic minority backgrounds, often for refugees, to advocacy, community or condition-specific groups to assist them in accessing healthcare, including provision of translators and interpreters.'CEMVO provides a bridge between patients and medical advisers. We liaise with doctors to ensure that clients' needs are understood and met. 'We do research for clients about what hospitals might meet their cultural and language needs. Patients could be signposted to expert patient programmes and other patient support groups and providers, for example voluntary sector social care providers that might have ethnic specialism.'

ippr/Health Link interview with CEMVO

'We employ bilingual workers. We require an expert on health, but we have links and could develop such advice services.

'BME [black and minority ethnic] people need help with form filling or they need to be accompanied to see GPs. There is a great unmet need from BME communities for health information in their own languages. Because of the language barriers, BME people require signposting, which FaithRegen could undertake.

'There are many cultural barriers in the NHS which we could help address, for example the need for same sex doctors.

'We could discuss outcomes and implications with clients and help them through advocacy. FaithRegen would be eager to work in health, but we would require funding to move into this area. We would suggest the best way is to start through pilot projects.'

ippr/Health Link interview with FaithRegen, ethnic minority and immigrant community organisation

'Our clients require interpreters – they use 42 different languages and therefore accessible translation and interpreting services are a priority, especially if people have to go to hospitals for follow-up treatment. Health advocates need to understand homeless people and their difficulties.'

ippr/Health Link interview with Broadway

> 'We sometimes have non-English speaking clients from black and minority ethnic groups. Unfortunately as a small local organisation we do not have translation services. We should have access to translation services like Language Line so that we can provide advice to all groups in the community.'
>
> ippr/Health Link interview with Alzheimer's Society branch

Learning disabilities

Patients with learning disabilities are also an underserved and high need group, with worse health outcomes and less healthcare provision for their needs than other patients. This reflects a range of factors, including poverty, unemployment and a lack of control over diet and exercise choices. People with learning disabilities also suffer from worse access to healthcare services. The government has acknowledged that they have not benefited proportionately from increases in health spending and from National Service Frameworks (Valuing People Support Team, 2005). At present people with learning disabilities are frequently not offered the same opportunities as other patients. The Healthcare Commission (2005) reported that policies to give people more control are less developed for people with learning disabilities.

The government has begun to implement its strategy for learning disability, *Valuing People* (DH 2001). This set out the objective to enable people with learning disabilities to have as much choice and control as possible over their lives through advocacy and a person-centred approach to planning the services and support they need. The challenge of involving people with learning disabilities will increase as choice is developed. Rather than leaving this high need group out of choice, more investment in training for professionals and support and advocacy for users needs to be provided. The voluntary sector organisation interviewed for this report argued that health advocacy provision was miniscule, and that advocacy in social services should also be provided to help people with learning disabilities access healthcare.

> 'Mencap could run projects to help patients express their preferences, for example using life books that explain what their needs are. We could set up local advocacy for patients with learning disabilities to support them in making choices. Advocacy has to be mainstreamed; there is currently only miniscule provision of health advocacy. 'Mencap could also provide education and training for clients, parents, family, care home staff and health workers on supporting people to make choices

> 'The NHS needs to develop accessible hospital information, learning from accessible health promotion initiatives.
>
> 'Transport is also a big barrier to accessing healthcare. People with learning disabilities suffer from bullying on public transport. Patient or community transport services are over-used, inconvenient and slow. This group needs more and better services in the community so they don't have to travel so far.
>
> 'People with learning disabilities receive very poor services now, with the problems starting before they enter the health system. Real choice is important but the current reforms don't meet Mencap's key aims. It is more important improve access and to provide better accessible information and communication so that clients are involved in decision-making and understand their health needs and adhere to treatments.'
>
> ippr/Health Link interview with Mencap

Sensory impairment

People with sensory impairments, including hearing and vision impairments, also find it hard to access healthcare. Sign's campaign Reaching Deaf Minds has highlighted that deaf people have poor access to healthcare, particularly in primary care. There is no communication support for 60 per cent of GP appointments for the hearing impaired.

> Deaf people's mental wellbeing depends on good access to their GPs and to other health services.
>
> One in six deafblind people have avoided visiting their GP because communication was too difficult.
>
> Sign www.reachingdeafminds.org.uk

As choice develops, accessible information and communication with patients with sensory deprivation will become even more important, to ensure that providers are responsive to their needs. For people with visual impairment, provision of information and communications in accessible formats including Braille and audiotape should be made standard. The availability of Browsealoud on www.nhs.uk is a good start, but other comparative and practical information also needs to be accessible so that choice is available to all blind and visually impaired users.

People with sensory impairment also require communication support and advocacy. Organisations like Sign provide outreach and advocacy support for deaf people with mental health issues, and could help deaf people making choices.

> 'If choice is more widely available then deaf people need to be properly included so that they do not receive a third class service compared with hearing people. This means deaf aware advocates and gateway workers who understand deaf culture and can relate to the NHS and to deaf people.'
>
> ippr/Health Link interview with Sign

For people with hearing impairment, NHS Direct's framework agreement for interpretation also covers British Sign Language interpreters, who can be commissioned to help healthcare professionals communicate with deaf service users. Sign has also developed a computer programme (details at www.signhealth.com) that is available to PCTs and GPs that allows doctors, nurses or receptionists to communicate more effectively with deaf patients. Communication aids can be speech-enabled and translated into a range of languages, which could improve access for a wider range of sensory-impaired people as well as other patients for whom English is a second language. Tools of this kind should be used by PCTs, GP practices and other healthcare organisations to enable better communication and more informed decision-making.

Communication disabilities

Research by Byng et al (2003) commissioned by the Department of Health recommended that people with communication disability should be a 'tracer group' for health services to track how well they were involving patients in decision-making. They recommend training in disability aware-ness and communication skills for all healthcare staff to ensure all patients' communication needs are met across the service. The NHS Alliance recom-mended that speech and language therapists may be needed to support patients with communication difficulties to ensure they can access infor-mation and communicate their choices (NHS Alliance, 2004). This will be even more important when more choice is offered to patients.

The communication disability network Connect's 'Starters programme' demonstrates a patient-centred way of working with clients living with stroke and aphasia and their families to offer and support choice making about their therapy and support services (Long-term Medical Conditions Alliance, 2003). Participation in this programme, run in the voluntary sec-tor, has led to changes in the types of choices people make, for example more clients choose to access conversation groups and alternative therapy and support rather than more standard therapy such as developing com-munication skills. This is a good example of how the voluntary sector can support difficult and disadvantaged choosers in taking a more active role in their healthcare decisions.

Mental health

People with mental health needs are often excluded from involvement in decisions about their care. The mental health patients' survey found nearly 60 per cent of mental health service users would like more involvement in decisions about their care, significantly more than in other areas of healthcare. The Healthcare Commission (2005) concluded that involvement of people with mental health needs has improved, but there is still some way to go. People with mental health problems have suffered stigma, poor practice and an underlying belief that patients are unable to make choices. Mental health policy and discussion have also been dominated by risk management and coercion agendas, rather than empowerment and patient centredness (Rankin, 2005).

Mental health services are not currently included in policies to extend choice. Rather than excluding mental health service users from choice and control over their services, it is more important that advice and advocacy are provided to people with mental health problems. Poor mental health is associated with perceived lack of autonomy, so it is even more important that people with mental health problems are empowered and supported to make more decisions about their services and providers, going beyond choice of provider to choice of treatments. A recent ippr report argues that greater choice and patient empowerment should be provided to patients using mental health services, including providing individual budgets so that service users can choose 'talking therapies' rather than prescribed drugs chosen for them by doctors. There is a significant user movement in mental health, which could be drawn on to support people in making choices, and independent advocates should support people in their interactions with professionals and advise on choices (Rankin, 2005).

Information and support for wider choices

'Choice is not only about episodes or spells of care and the choice not to wait to access care, it is also about providing choices that are based on the whole person. Without this "whole person" approach, the choice initiative will become meaningless.'

NHS Alliance, 2004

By improving resources and information brokerage in the VCS, patient choice support policies could improve healthy social capital (Barber and Gordon-Dseagu, 2003). Poor health is partly determined by social networks – people with more social and community interactions are less likely to suffer poor health (and vice versa). By engaging patient and community organisations in providing support for healthcare choices, the policies proposed in this report could improve people's social wellbeing and contribute to reduce health inequalities.

An evaluation of the choice project in Greater Manchester found that 51 per cent of people who did not take up choice had had no opportunity to discuss their choice with others, for example friends, family or community networks (Barber et al, 2004). Social capital and ability to make informed choice are already linked, so policies to improve equitable choices should also aim to improve social capital. By investing in VCS organisations to provide information and support for choice, these policies will improve the capacity of this sector and encourage people to get involved in community organisations, including but not exclusively those that are health-related. Choice support policy would then contribute to building healthy social capital among disadvantaged groups that are more at risk of social exclusion.

VCS organisations find it difficult to influence the health system. Health system decision-making is seen as inaccessible and bureaucratic. The use of VCS organisations will improve their capacity to engage with the NHS. This would help to join up the individual 'choice' policies and the wider collective 'voice' agenda. Rather than being in conflict, choice supported by VCS organisations could encourage and empower people to get involved in collective decision-making and public involvement. In order to do this, patients who receive information, support or advocacy in the community would be given a 'stake' or a 'share' in that organisation and would be invited to get involved in the public engagement opportunities that VCS organisations could secure.

A wider facilitated network of public involvement, capitalising on the increased importance of the VCS in supporting patient choice, should be developed to establish a much bigger critical mass of interest and activity in health. This could in turn boost the power and activism of patient and public involvement forums, providing people who might not normally get involved with an opportunity, through taking part in choice, to participate in decision-making about local health services.

The capacity of the VCS, including funding, is a challenge to delivering choice support. Guidance and codes have been provided to improve the way the statutory sector works with the VCS, but concerns remain about their implementation, as highlighted by the Social Exclusion Unit (2005). The SEU highlights good practice on partnership working, including co-location. Organisations contributing to choice and public involvement need opportunities for more reliable long-term sources of income so they can invest in resources and training to meet the needs of disadvantaged groups. The Better Partnerships Task Force recommended a specific work programme to reduce the administrative burdens associated with funding (2005). Voluntary and community organisations may also need to improve their skills in bidding for and managing larger contracts.

PCTs will have to commit resources to information, support and advocacy whilst ensuring that the VCS delivers value for money. Although it is necessary for commissioners to balance this need against other priorities, if good quality information support and advocacy are neglected then inequities will increase and disadvantaged groups will be left behind, with longer-term health and social costs.

Access and geography

At present healthcare inequities due to unequal abilities to access and understand information are compounded by inequitable provision of services across the country. This is one of the reasons for introducing more choice of providers. With patient choice, geographical inequity could be reduced by allowing patients to access providers outside their geographical area and, as discussed in the next chapter, by possibly incentivising poor providers to improve.

There are concerns that people in rural areas in particular will have less access to choice than people in urban areas. At present, use of, experience and satisfaction with healthcare (pre-choice) may actually be the same or better in rural areas than in towns and cities (Buchanan, 2004). Quantitative research on the accessibility of alternative acute providers has shown that there are variations across England in terms of access to alternative providers (Damiani et al, 2005) due to distance or lack of spare capacity. If people are not going to be disadvantaged by where they live, there should be increased investment in alternative providers in those under-served areas. Alternatively, extra transport support for patient in those areas should be provided so that they can access a wider range of choices. New entrants into the health market should be incentivised and regulated to ensure that they equalise rather than exacerbate geographical inequities in access to choice.

Access and transport

Geographic access is less significant than access to transport in current healthcare inequities (Dixon et al, 2003). Access to transport, particularly

---

Transport and health access – key facts

■ Three per cent of people, or 1.4 million, miss, turn down or do not seek healthcare because of lack of access to transport.

■ This rises to 5-6 per cent in deprived wards and 7 per cent in car-less households.

■ Seventeen per cent of people with a car find it difficult to travel to hospital. A much higher proportion (31 per cent) of people without access to a car have this difficulty.

> - Eighty-nine per cent of the least deprived decile travel to hospital by car, compared with 56 per cent of the most deprived decile.
>
> - Between 23 and 25 per cent of people in small towns and 11 per cent of people in rural areas live in car-less households.
>
> - More over-75s find access to local hospital difficult than any other age group.
>
> Social Exclusion Unit (2003); Office of National Statistics (2005)

car ownership, is associated with better health outcomes.

Patient choice may alleviate some of the inequities in access to healthcare caused by transport inequalities. By allowing people to choose and book an appointment time and location, people will be able to arrange their healthcare around the availability of public transport, or when a carer could provide transport for them. However, this will not alleviate all transport-related inequity. More importantly, if disadvantaged groups are limited by transport then they will not have an equitable access to choice. Patients choosing on the basis of practicalities to do with transport will not be able to choose on the basis of quality and could end up with sink services. Higher personal transport costs could lead to differences in waiting times, with poorer people having to wait longer (Bugess et al, 2005).

The role of transport in determining whether people are able to participate in patient choice has been demonstrated in choice pilots and analysis of surveys. Free and/or organised transport to alternative providers was piloted in the choice at six months projects and factored into surveys. Payment for, or even just the arrangement of transport by the NHS, had a positive impact on take-up of choice in London (Burge et al, 2005). Transport costs excluded some low income or unemployed people from choice in Greater Manchester, where transport was not offered to all (Barber et al, 2004).

> **Transport and choice – key facts**
> - Travel is the key factor for many older people in whether they would take up choice (40 per cent of over-75s).
>
> - Older people, working class people and non-car owners are less likely to travel further to an alternative provider.
>
> - Over 80 per cent of older people are prepared to travel to a different hospital for quicker treatment if transport is provided free of charge.
>
> - Poorer patients trade off quality against distance more than wealthier patients.
>
> - Distance to alternative hospitals was more important for those who did not take up choice.
>
> MORI (2003); Help the Aged (2003); Burge et al (2005)

The government has not fully recognised the importance of transport in equalising access to choice. In the national roll-out of choice at referral, free transport will only be provided for those groups already entitled to it. The NHS currently runs two schemes to help with transport to healthcare. Non-emergency Patient Transport Service (PTS) is an ambulance service provided by hospitals to bring from their home to hospital people who have been classified as having medical need for transport. The Hospital Travel Costs Scheme (HTCS) refunds the cost of transport to patients who are claiming certain benefits or tax credits. Both schemes have been strongly criticised by Citizens Advice (2001), the Audit Commission (2001) and the Social Exclusion Unit (2003) for being inequitably provided across the country, difficult to access and failing to tackle the transport barriers to healthcare.

The Social Exclusion Unit announced in 2003 that the government would reform these schemes so that free transport services would be available to people with a social need, and would be made more accessible. As yet the Department of Health has not implemented these agreed policies. Citizens Advice is still concerned that transport remains an important barrier to access to healthcare. Help the Aged and Mencap have also suggested that, for disadvantaged groups, transport is a major obstacle to accessing choice of provider (ippr interviews 2005). The evaluations of the London Patient Choice Project warned that failure to arrange or pay for transport to alternative choices will reduce the take-up of choice. This will have a disproportionate effect on car-less households, lower socio-economic groups, older people and many parents and carers.

If choice is to be available to all then the policies on provision of transport to healthcare should be reformed. The government and the NHS should use the data from previous trials and other available data to work out which groups are in greatest need of transport assistance in order to access choice. Patients in car-less households where public transport is inadequate or difficult for them to use (for example due to disability, frailness or dependents) should be prioritised to receive free and arranged transport. Some groups might only need support in arranging transport; other groups may be able to use and arrange transport but need more straightforward ways of claiming back expenses or be sent a travel pass or payment voucher if preferred.

The government and the NHS will have two to three years to develop better transport arrangements for choice between five providers. When free choice of providers is introduced in 2008, the policy will have to be adapted to respond to a possible (but not inevitable) increase in the need for transport to more distant providers. However, in the meantime, choice should also be developed to improve services in the community, with options for services offered outside hospital, as explored in chapter four.

Provision of transport obviously has a cost for the healthcare budget. However, there could be initial efficiency gains if the number of missed appointments reduce. A courtesy car service for patients at Doncaster and Bassetlaw NHS Foundation Trust (supported by WRVS) has been found to be cost-effective (Foundation Trust Network, 2005). Transport costs may be charged to the chosen hospital rather than to the PCT as this would incentivise providers to offer care closer to the patient. If choice and practice-based commissioning succeed in shifting care outside hospitals then the distances to travel could be reduced, so transport costs may not be so high.

In a whole person-centred model of healthcare, the social needs of patients are also important, so getting a patient to the location of preferred treatment may be as important as the care he or she receives once there. Where the transport divide contributes to healthcare inequalities, there are health and social justice arguments for providing subsidised and supported transport. The government has neglected this issue, and the implementation of choice creates an added impetus to implement reform to healthcare transport.

Conclusion

Patients in the NHS are currently unequally involved in decision-making. This is due to a range of factors, including health literacy, language, education, disabilities, and digital exclusion.

Choice has been piloted in several areas and specialties. The London project had positive equity findings, with disadvantaged groups participating in choice as much as other groups. However, the pilots have limited applicability to the choice policies that are being rolled out, and choice at referral has not been evaluated for its impact on equity of access to choice, access to services or outcomes. Whilst choice pilots have successfully delivered more equitable 'choosability' using PCAs and transport as well as incentives for providers these important lessons have not been implemented in the roll-out of choice. The impact of choice on equity should be evaluated as it is rolled out and extra support be targeted to groups that are detected as being disadvantaged.

Patients need to have access to information in order to make choices. This information must be easily available and measure health-related quality of life outcomes. Other areas of patient experience must be included so that patients can make choices based on their particular needs and preferences. Independent sector providers should be subject to the same information requirements as NHS providers so that patients can have comparable information with which to make choices.

Disadvantaged groups in particular require support and advocacy to take part in choice. Support and advocacy should be commissioned from a range of sources, particularly from patient groups and other voluntary and community organisations such as Citizens Advice that have good relationships with disadvantaged groups. Patients should be able to choose their source of information and support, and GPs could provide 'support prescriptions' for patients who might need targeted advice or advocacy.

The provision of advice should be commissioned and regulated to ensure that high standards are maintained and disadvantaged groups are included. PCTs will need to balance their spending priorities so that enough resources are available to commission effective information support and advocacy.

People without access to a car, who are often disadvantaged and with greater health needs, are currently disadvantaged in access to health services. Choice pilots demonstrated that transport acted as a barrier to accessing chosen healthcare services. Provision of transport, assistance with organising transport or subsidy of the cost should be reviewed so that less mobile people are not excluded from choice.

3
Equity, contestability and voice

The previous chapter discussed how choice should be implemented equitably, ensuring that all patients, particularly those from disadvantaged groups, have equal opportunity to access healthcare and make choices about treatment, self-care and healthy life choices. We suggested some ways for this to be achieved.

However, concerns about equity of choice go beyond ability and willingness to choose. Although this report argues that choice should be developed in order to empower disadvantaged patients, the major driver for introducing choice has been to create contestability between providers (Catton, 2005). In this chapter, we argue that increasing 'quasi-market' incentives can pose a number of challenges and opportunities for equity. This report does not aim to tackle the question of whether markets should be introduced in public services. We examine how choice policy should be implemented in order to ensure that inequalities are not worsened and we make recommendations to that effect.

The introduction of choice of provider in secondary care is the mechanism being used by the government to create more 'contestability' between providers. By financing providers according to the number of patients who choose to have their operation there, the traditional mechanism of centrally-allocated budgets and block contracts with PCTs will be replaced with a different financial framework. Providers will have to compete to attract patients.

'Payment by Results' (PbR) is the new financial system accompanying 'choose and book'. A national tariff of fixed prices for each procedure, adjusted for complexity where appropriate, will be allocated according to the number of patients who choose, at point of referral, to go to each provider. The higher costs in more expensive parts of the country will be subsidised centrally according to the 'market forces factor'. Private and voluntary sector providers will be able to enter the healthcare market if they charge tariff prices and meet national standards regulated by the Healthcare Commission. The aim is mainly to create incentives for NHS and other providers to improve efficiency, quality and responsiveness to meet patients' needs and preferences. Providers chosen by a higher number of patients will be able to expand and receive more patients and more payments. Services that are unpopular or loss-making will have to improve quality and responsiveness to attract more patients, or improve their efficiency. Some services and providers may have to contract or even close.

This new system may affect equity in a number of ways. By creating contestability, it could lead to 'polarisation' of providers, with a few hospitals attracting more patients (and funding) so that they improve and expand, while other providers enter a spiral of decline with fewer patients and less funding. This may increase geographical inequity and leave some areas with 'sink' providers with limited services and lower quality. If patients are unable or unwilling to choose to travel further to alternative providers, this would lead to inequity, with patients who live in an area with poorer quality or limited services receiving poorer care.

The new quasi-market could also create inequitable perverse incentives for providers actively to select or more subtly to attract patients who are cheaper to treat. If the price-setting system is poorly designed some services could become more profitable, which could lead to a disproportionate investment and provision of those services, and a decline in services for less 'profitable' procedures, disadvantaging patients with particular under-priced problems. If patients are differently able or willing to choose, then this could place greater incentives on providers to meet the needs and preferences of only the active choosers, thereby reducing the effort to meet the needs of those less willing or able to choose.

Contestability and polarisation

Perhaps the greatest concern about contestability in healthcare provision is that it will lead to a 'two-tier' health service (Perri 6, 2003; Appleby et al, 2003). Competition leads to winners and losers. This has been emphasised by politicians, who have said that hospitals would be allowed to close if they were performing badly and patients were not choosing them, or if they were not able to provide services at the tariff price (BBC, 2005a; BBC, 2005b). Patients living near 'declining' hospitals, who are less willing or able to travel further for their healthcare, would then receive poor quality or more limited services. The effect of polarisation could be to increase healthcare inequities and worsen health inequalities.

Polarisation would not inevitably increase inequity. The present NHS hospital provision is not geographically equitable (Damiani et al, 2005). Also, quality is not equally distributed across the country, with variations measured in waiting times, surgical death rates or health outcomes. However, the fact that there is currently inequity does not mean that potentially increasing polarisation does not matter.

An important aim for health system reforms should be to reduce variations as part of a general desire to improve quality. Responsiveness, innovation and efficiency are actually stated as the primary objectives of choice and contestability (DH, 2004c). Patients will be able to choose the hospital that provides the best service to meet their needs and preferences and poor providers are expected to improve. For patients in areas with poor quality or longer waiting times, choice could reduce the effect of existing geographical inequity in provision.

However, as the previous chapter showed, the take-up of choice among disadvantaged groups may be lower than among more mobile patients and those who are more able to access and process information. Although ability to choose is not inevitably determined by socio-economic status, evidence from pilots found that older and poorer people are more likely to trade off quality against travel time. If contestability leads to polarisation then there will be even more urgency for the government and the NHS to implement our recommendations. These would ensure that choice is available to all so that they can access the higher quality providers, and the already disadvantaged do not become even more so.

Evidence of polarisation

Choice is also intended to improve the quality of providers that are not chosen as well as those that are, by providing strong incentives to attract patients. In the London Patient Choice Project (LPCP), patients at Originating Trusts (OTs), with longer waiting times, were able to choose a Receiving Trust (RT) with a shorter wait. An evaluation of LPCP found that the performance of OTs improved as they lost patients (Dawson et al, 2005). Even allowing for the extra investment in capacity in London and falling waiting times across the country, for most choice specialties waiting times at OTs fell significantly faster than in the rest of the country, whilst RTs also reduced their waiting times. Waiting times for patients who did not choose were reduced, so choice did not just benefit the 'choosers'. If this performance-driving effect can be reproduced in the national implementation of choose and book, then concerns about polarisation and left behind services may be assuaged.

However, this evaluation of LPCP sounded a warning about the transferability of lessons from the pilots. As discussed, choice at referral is fundamentally different to choice at six months, with the aim being that patients choose on the basis of responsiveness and quality rather than just on waiting times.

Because choice at referral has not been so extensively piloted it is difficult to predict its real effect. The government may have under-estimated the effect of choice on the stability of hospitals. In its report on the preparations for choose and book, the National Audit Office noted that the government's predictive modelling suggested that the impact of choice on healthcare providers would be mediated by waiting times. Waiting time would act as a 'makeweight' that so that over-prescribed hospitals would increase waiting times and patients would choose other providers (National Audit Office, 2005). However, this effect probably applies more in the current climate of waiting times than it would post-2008 when no one is supposed to wait more than 18 weeks. If this target is achieved then the volatility of the market (and the risk of polarisation) will be increased. Another 'makeweight' to prevent polarisation could be that sicker patients are concentrated in higher quality hospitals (Burgess et al, 2005), improving outcomes for those patients but averaging out measured performance across the system and allowing poorer quality hospitals to improve by investing their income from less severe patients.

It is estimated that a relatively small churn of patients switching providers would be enough to create incentives for providers (Appleby, 2005). However, this would conflict with equity objectives. Our progressive vision of patient choice goes beyond choice being a means to the end of creating contestability. Choice should aim to empower and engage disadvantaged groups in healthcare, requiring that the greatest number of patients as possible should have the opportunity to choose whilst also ensuring that service standards are improved in unchosen providers rather than allowing them to fall into a spiral of decline.

In order for the incentive effect of contestability to be real, there needs to be a real – or perceived – threat that failing to meet patients' needs and preferences will lead to financial sanctions. If unchosen providers are propped up with debt cancellations and support funds, then the incentive effect will be weaker. However, if there is no flexibility or support for the unchosen they could be perversely incentivised to make short-term cuts to services or standards in order to survive financially. This would lead to a cycle of decline and polarisation which harms patients, staff and the health system.

Regulation and equity

Contestability may lead to changes in service levels, with providers expanding and contracting, entering and, sometimes, closing down services that are no longer viable. Market exit (the closure or reduction of departments or providers) should not be allowed to reduce quality and access for patients. In particular, as choice and PbR are rolled out, local risk management strategies should be permitted while the new system is bedding in, in order to maintain the stability of the local health economy and patient services (Audit Commission, 2005). There may in time be scenarios where closure can work in favour of patients. Where patients have abandoned a service due to existing and intractable poor quality, closure of that service would be necessary to protect patients, as is currently the case with any service that is not meeting minimum Healthcare Commission standards.

One of the aims of patient choice is to improve allocative efficiency by exposing services that are inefficient or providing services for which there is insufficient demand. In a scenario where patient choice reveals excess capacity and there is an alternative provider that is providing the same service more efficiently and maintaining quality standards, it could be in the interest of both patients and the health service for services to close. We should recognise that the status quo does not represent the optimal distribution of services and, as equity studies have shown, current provision does not serve the poorest communities best.

Regulation and market management will have an important role to play in ensuring that contestability does not increase inequities. In the first instance, the role of healthcare regulation is to ensure minimum standards and drive improvement. Regulators will continue to protect patients from services that fall below minimum standards.

PCTs and strategic health authorities need to ensure that local populations have access to adequate levels of quality services according to need. The decision to allow a provider or a department to close should therefore be taken based on assurance that closure will not reduce the availability of service for local populations according to need. Market management needs to be based on clear patient-centred criteria. Rather than leaving providers to 'sink or swim' in a free market of patient choice, a scale of supportive interventions should be targeted at providers that are at risk of falling into decline. The involvement of patients and the public in decisions about closures and reconfigurations should be prioritised. Where patients and the public have not been effectively consulted, as in Kidderminster, reconfigurations have proved extremely unpopular although standards and access to care did not fall (Raftery and Harris, 2005). However, where effective consultation has been carried out, for example using citizens' juries, service reconfigurations have successfully met patients' needs and engaged the public in democratic decision-making (Hewitt, 2005; Parkinson, 2003).

Closure should be discouraged in less densely populated or less well served areas, unless the local population can be guaranteed that new providers will be able to ensure those services are replaced. Tied up with the regulation of market exit is the regulation and stimulation of market entry. In order for contestability to lead to more responsive levels of service, new providers will have to enter the market to fill gaps of unmet need and replace sub-standard providers. New providers could also enter the market to increase competitiveness in areas or specialties where there is currently little choice. Whilst the economics of market entry and exit has not been the main focus of this project, it is clear that managing the new market will be necessary and the stated principles of market regulation should be established, prioritising the need to ensure equity for disadvantaged patients.

Proposed principles for market management and regulation

- Hospitals and services should only be allowed to close if interventions have been made in order to support and improve the service.

- The withdrawal of the service should not reduce patients' access to services according to need.

- An alternative existing or new provider should reasonably be able to serve the patients who were using the service.

- Removal of a service should not reduce the competitiveness of the local health economy. Expansion of existing providers should also be regulated to prevent uncompetitive monopolies.

- Current or future users of the service should be supported to access the alternative provider if they are further away by providing free transport to more distant providers.

- Market regulation should involve patients and the public in setting standards and making local decisions. In particular, VCS organisations serving and representing disadvantaged groups should be consulted.

- Market entry regulation also needs to be based on clear principles. New providers should reflect the needs and preferences of local populations.

- All providers should be encouraged to provide innovative services to meet patient needs and preferences. In particular, patients should be offered a choice of a provider of care outside hospitals closer to patients.

- Market entry by niche providers needs to be monitored to ensure that they do not have unfair advantages. Externalities such as intensive care back-up and training should therefore be factored into payments.

- All providers treating NHS patients should have a 'duty to treat' to prevent provider selection. However, this should not compromise either patient safety, for example where a complex patient requires intensive care, or training needs.

- All providers should be subject to equitable regulation to ensure a level playing field. Private and voluntary sector providers should provide the same information for choice as NHS providers. NHS Trusts should not be disadvantaged by their responsibilities as public sector employers and trainers.

Market regulation will also need to address potential problems created by imperfect pricing and quality information. Some critics of choice and PbR have pointed out that inflexible tariffs could create incentives for providers to play the system by selecting patients who might be cheaper to treat and therefore more 'profitable' (British Medical Association, 2004; Burgess et al, 2005; Public Administration Select Committee, 2005). This could worsen inequities if more complex patients, for example older patients or those with co-morbidities, are 'skimped' (ie under-treated) or 'dumped' (ie not accepted for treatment). Since these issues were raised, the government has continued to develop PbR to be more responsive to the complexity of patients, and to counteract possible games, for example by increasing the number of codes for each procedure to reflect complexities, and paying daily costs for patients who have complications that require longer post-operative care (DH 2004e). The government also needs to balance the need to reflect actual costs with the need to keep the system simple and un-bureaucratic. Gaming is possible in any system, and the organisations working with PbR need to respect the values of fairness and equity. The government should emphasise this in the forthcoming code of conduct for PbR (DH 2005d).

Opportunities for selection of patients by providers should also be minimised by enforcing a 'duty to treat' policy, within the parameters of patient safety. Furthermore, evidence suggests that patients might be more motivated to choose higher quality providers if they are more sick. As discussed in chapter two, patients in more pain were more likely to opt to go to an alternative provider in the LPCP (Coulter et al, 2005). Whilst this might apply more for choice at six months, analysis of treatment given to older Medicare patients in the US found that competitiveness increased the appropriateness of treatment, with sicker patients receiving more intensive treatment than healthier ones (Burgess et al, 2005). Competition could, therefore, improve equity of treatment according to need. This should not be taken as guaranteed, however, and it is important that the government and regulators monitor the effects of competition on appropriateness of treatment.

One additional risk is that, by reducing the role of clinicians in prioritising referrals according to need, patients referred for the same procedure but with different levels of need will have equal (but inequitable) waiting times and quality (Appleby et al, 2003). This may be an acceptable trade-off between equity and efficiency if quality is well regulated and total waiting times are within safe parameters, as is the target by 2008. It should be noted that for very time-contingent conditions such as cancer or emergency treatment, patient choice will not be used, as the priority is early assessment and treatment. Again, these effects should be monitored and evaluated, including the extent to which different groups trade off waiting time, quality and proximity. Options to mediate inequity due to lack of prioritisation might include providing patients with a priority level that would be taken into account by the choose and book system.

Support and collaboration

In order to ensure that patient choice leads to improvement rather than polarisation into high quality and sink services, the government and the NHS should put in place mechanisms to support and improve 'failing' providers, particularly where there is high demand. Whilst incentivising good performance, the government should provide support, in the form of longer-term budgets, loans and expertise in order to improve rather than allow providers to decline.

One option would be to allow successful providers to run services within other providers, offering a mid-way between merging and collaborating. This idea of franchising services has been experimented. One foundation trust, Moorfields Eye Hospital, has already opened up franchises across London to provide ophthalmology services in other hospitals, although this was to improve access and efficiency for a specialist service (Foundation Trust Network, 2005) rather than due to failing competitors. This could radically change the way that hospitals are run, more as boutiques or franchised services than as separate institutions. This could have advantages by ensuring that 'failing' services are improved, and encouraging better sharing of information and expertise between organisations. However, it could also involve risks by creating monopolies and over-powerful large providers, which could dominate markets, thereby reducing efficiency, patient choice and primary care led services. Where natural monopolies emerge there will have to be alternative methods to ensure there is sufficient choice within providers and incentives to improve. Franchising needs to be evaluated before being spread further, but if well supported and regulated then it could provide an alternative to polarisation.

Patient choice and voice

Providers that ignore the needs and preferences of patients and the public will not be chosen, and as a result will lose patients, funding and services. If money follows the patient then hospitals will not be able to afford to ignore patients' voices. Therefore in order for patient choice to work, patient and public involvement needs to turn a corner and be established at the heart of healthcare decision-making. The collective voice of patients' choices needs to be heard.

In order for the quasi-market to work, providers need to respond rapidly to consumer demands. Providers and commissioners need to have a sophisticated understanding of what patients are choosing and why, so that they can meet those needs.

Some providers have already begun to recognise this. Some Foundation Trusts have engaged market research and public involvement consultants to survey their potential market to find out what they want from their health services, and on what basis they will make their choice of provider. These providers can attract patients by offering them the services they prefer, and will be able to respond to their needs. This kind of practice, of finding out what patients want, will be the key to the success of providers. It is important that all providers invest in finding out what patients want, and that these skills are mainstreamed in the NHS. The NHS should use its bulk-purchasing ability to negotiate lower costs for market research, for example by procuring national contracts that can be called-off at a local level.

Market research is not the only way that the voice of choice can be heard. Patients and the public should be involved as consumer-citizens in decision-making, in particular in designing services that meet their needs and preferences. As discussed in the previous chapter, healthcare commissioners and providers need to make much greater use of patient groups and other local voluntary and community organisations. These groups possess a wealth of untapped knowledge about their clients' preferences and experiences. Providers and commissioners and voluntary and community groups should liaise and share this information so that services can be tailored to meet patients' needs. Through this process providers will benefit by acquiring knowledge, improving services and thereby attracting patients. Patients will benefit as services and providers will become more responsive to their needs. This type of collective influencing enhances the role of the VCS and ultimately enhances the often-unheard voice of disadvantaged patients.

At present, understanding patient and public needs and preferences is not a priority for commissioners and providers. Consultation with patients and the public has been made a legal obligation on NHS bodies by the Health and Social Care Act 2002. However, in the context of national targets and other reforms, many in the NHS and public and patient involvement field do not feel that this has been enough of a priority. VCS organisations interviewed by ippr and Health Link still find that influencing local health services is bureaucratic and ineffective. There is widespread frustration, and a belief that current public and patient involvement policies are not achieving their aims. Members of the public who are involved in healthcare, for example as non-executive directors or patient and public involvement forum members, do not tend to represent the most disadvantaged groups. The Commission for Health Improvement (CHI) found that 'Patient and public involvement (PPI) is not yet having a major impact on policy and practice. This is despite a plethora of PPI initiatives. It is almost as if there is a brick wall between the activities going on and any changes on the ground that happen as a result' (CHI, 2004).

> 'I doubt how much influence we really have. There is so much paperwork for these meetings that you feel that things are slipped through that you don't spot. It feels like change is driven by government policy, with local organisations worried about complying with a new piece of legislation, rather than working in partnership to find better ways to use resources to meet needs/preferences of clients. If it feels like this for a relatively experienced worker how must it feel for users or carer representatives?'
>
> ippr/Health Link interview with Alzheimer's Society branch

Involving patient groups and VCS organisations in supporting patient choice would facilitate improved public involvement and allow the voices and experiences of disadvantaged groups to be represented. Organisations brokering information and supporting choice should obtain feedback from users on what they want from their healthcare providers. This would include recording why they chose the provider they opted for and suggesting what else they would have liked.

Organisations supporting patients in this process should also collate feedback from patients about their experiences of providers. This would provide a rich source of real intelligence for local commissioners and providers. Rather than losing patients due to failure to meet their preferences and falling into a spiral of declining income and quality, providers would be able to find out why patients were choosing alternative providers and then address those aspects of the service. Providing real market and community intelligence in this way would close the loop of choice and contestability. It would show that collective 'voice' is needed to complement individual choice. Our research, in partnership with Health Link, found that patient and community organisations are well placed to develop this role, and there is a desire – subject to resources – to contribute to delivering equitable choices and influencing services to meet the needs of patients (see box).

'We would be collecting evidence of outcomes and could feed into the NHS to improve services. We would need funding to recruit and train people to give such health advice. Our experience in work brokerage would be a good starting point, since communication is so important in employment and in health.'

ippr/Health Link interview with FaithRegen

'Our role in supporting patients in making choices could help to influence local health services if we had the capacity to feed patients' experiences into the NHS planning and commissioning process. If we tracked the patients we supported we could glean quality information. We would need a lot of funding for this to happen because this is time consuming work. Not only would we need to keep tabs on people but we would also have to develop close working relationships with the providers and commissioners of healthcare to enable us to give this feedback.'

ippr/Health Link interview with Sign

'Patients going through the system should complete evaluation and feedback forms to help evaluate and monitor decisions. It is important that choice focuses on meeting needs rather than glossy advertising, especially with more use of private sector providers that are less accountable.'

ippr/Health Link interview with CEMVO

> 'If we had time for report writing and submitting the findings, it
> could contribute to learning. Normally we support our clients to
> help themselves so we might support them to give feedback on their
> experiences with the NHS directly to the NHS.'
>
> ippr/Health Link interview with ATD 4th World

By ensuring that disadvantaged groups are particularly supported, and
the voice of their choices is particularly well heard, these proposals would
ensure that providers respond to their needs and preferences. In this way
individual choices become collective forces for service improvement for
patients, driving a patient-led health service.

Amplifying the voice of disadvantage patients by linking them with
support and advocacy in the community would help ensure that providers
do not compete to attract only the 'posh and pushy' well-connected middle class patients. By ensuring that patients choose on the basis of quality
information, perverse incentives to compete by 'glossy marketing' would
be reduced.

As well as spreading choice to disadvantaged groups, stimulating local
community organisations could improve health, reduce health inequalities
and contribute to tackling social exclusion. Putting the act of choosing in
a collective, community context would allow users to choose as citizens
as well as individual consumers. Users would be able to meet other users,
and access peer networks and self-care support. By pooling their individual
choices in the community, patients could claim collective power to influence public services to meet their needs.

Conclusions

Choice has been introduced in order to create contestability between providers, with the aim of improving quality and responsiveness. This has
potential risks for equity, particularly if competition leads to polarisation,
for example through service closures leaving areas under-served.

Market management by commissioners and effective regulation must
ensure that the operation of this market does not reduce choice, and does
not create sink services for patients who are less mobile. Market entry and
exit should be managed and regulated according to principles of protect-
ing equity and ensuring fair competition. Providers that are losing patients
need to be supported to ensure that essential services are maintained and
they improve their services to meet patients' needs and preferences.

Voluntary and community organisations that provide information, support and advice for disadvantaged groups should also gather intelligence
on people's reasons for choosing, and on their experiences of providers.
This information should be fed back to providers and commissioners so

that services reflect patient requirements. Providers and commissioners will need to engage with communities more effectively to ensure their needs and preferences are being met.

Voluntary and community organisations, as well as good quality market research, will therefore provide information which ensures services respond to patients' voices, particularly the most disadvantaged. This progressive vision would create a more patient-led NHS, with powerful collective voice backed up by the financial force of choice and PbR.

4
Equitable choices in primary care

We have explored how access to choice should be extended to everyone, particularly disadvantaged patients who are currently under-served. We argue that choice should be linked to wider health improvement and public involvement agendas. We have also recommended how the secondary care market should be managed to benefit disadvantaged groups, involving VCS organisations in feeding back the collective voice of choice to ensure that disadvantaged groups are heard and involved in service design and configuration.

Secondary care has for too long enjoyed most of the focus of government policy. If progressive goals of improving health and reducing health inequalities are to be achieved, the focus of policy-makers should be on ensuring that preventative and early intervention services are improved so that people's health does not deteriorate to the point when they need to go to hospital. If policies to encourage empowerment, health literacy, self-care and improving the choice and voice of disadvantaged patients is limited to secondary care referrals then the potential gains, and the contribution towards a 'fully engaged' scenario, will be missed. 'Full engagement' describes the scenario proposed by Wanless (2002) in which levels of public engagement, health status and NHS responsiveness are high, and the benefits of investment are maximised.

Choice in primary care

At the time of writing, the government is conducting a public consultation called *Your Health, Your Care, Your Say* to find out what people want from their community health and social care services. This will feed into a white paper to be published in winter 2005/06. Amongst the options being discussed in the consultation are how people can be supported to care for themselves, and how services can be delivered and co-ordinated closer to the community. We welcome the new emphasis being placed on primary health and social care as ippr has argued these are key areas for reaching disadvantaged patients and for preventing ill health in the first place. We hope that the consultation succeeds in reaching the most disadvantaged groups, which are currently under-served.

This chapter raises some of the key equity risks and opportunities in developing choice in primary care, and recommends some principles and practical options for reducing inequity. These issues have been explored in our research, discussions with experts and stakeholders, consultation with voluntary and community organisations and a private seminar held with senior policy-makers and experts.

Our discussions suggest that there is even more confusion about choice in primary care than in secondary care. Following consultation, the government needs to be clear what the priorities are for primary care reform and design policies to meet those aims, rather than again allowing contestability to drive the agenda. Choice should become part of the system of improvement, integrated with other drivers including inspection and commissioning. Primary care reform should aim to realise the vision of progressive choice that we have outlined in this report, aiming to improve services for the most disadvantaged, empowering patients and providing meaningful choices.

Equity and primary care

From an equity perspective the challenges for primary care are similar to those in the rest of the health system. Indeed, many of the problems of inequity in access to hospital services begin in primary care as people find it harder to seek primary care advice at an early stage, or fail to secure equitable referrals from their GP. People from lower socio-economic groups are more likely to go to accident and emergency departments as the first point of access, indicating barriers to accessing primary care in the community (Dixon et al, 2003). Dixon et al found that lower socio-economic groups may be consulting GPs as much as others but they may be receiving less benefit per consultation, and seeking care later. As equity is defined by need, different areas, different groups and individuals with different needs should receive appropriately differential services. So responsiveness should be a key aim of primary care reform.

Primary care suffers from a particular problem of capacity that has repercussions for the rest of the healthcare system. There is still an inverse care law in provision of GPs. Poorer areas are less likely to have as many health professionals, and people living in areas with higher levels of illness are more likely to spend more than 50 hours per week doing unpaid care (Wheeler et al, 2005). Despite financial inducements to open practices in under-provided areas, it has been estimated that 15 per cent of the population faces closed GP lists (DH, 2003b). This is a particular problem in London, where the 'inverse care law' is most strongly observable (Baker and Hann, 2001).

There are also equity problems with the registration system. Citizens advice bureaux deal with many cases where people have been removed from practice lists and have struggled against an unaccountable registration system. Some cases have reached the Health Service Ombudsman (2004). Socially excluded groups, including homeless people, people living in temporary accommodation, Travellers and Gypsies and asylum seekers are also often excluded by the registration system. For example, the Social Exclusion Unit (SEU) identified registration as a barrier to accessing services for disadvantaged adults who move frequently (SEU, 2005), and the Commission for Racial Equality (CRE) found that Travellers and Gypsies have difficulties in registration, leading to over-reliance on accident and emergency and less continuity of care (CRE, 2004).

Primary care affects equity in other ways. Dixon et al's (2003) review identified transport and work commitments as creating barriers to accessing GPs. Schemes for patient transport currently exclude primary care access, acting as a potential barrier to appropriate care for patients with mobility problems or lack of access to a car or public transport (SEU, 2003). Work commitments, particularly for workers who are more likely to be on short term contracts and/or hourly rates, are also a barrier to accessing healthcare (Dixon et al, 2003). Geographical restrictions on GP access are therefore a greater problem for people in lower paid and insecure jobs.

As discussed in chapter one, Dixon et al found that inequity in the NHS came from inequality in 'voice', being able to communicate with professionals and navigate the system, as well as inequalities in healthcare-seeking behaviour. The key to solving these problems lies not in secondary care but in developing choice in primary care. One of the aims of primary care should be to co-ordinate individual patients' care through the health system, acting as a gateway as well as a gatekeeper. This gateway role has been poorly developed, leading to inequity of service along the care pathway, and there is debate as to whether the GP is the best or only model for co-ordination of care (Saltman, 2005).

As discussed in this report, the progressive case for choice lies in empowering patients and improving health literacy, self-care and ability to navigate the system. Choice of secondary care provider and wider choice of treatment should be implemented in order to create a better dialogue between empowered, informed and supported patients and healthcare professionals. Implementing progressive, equitable choices throughout the health system could be helped by developing wider choice policies in primary care. This chapter will discuss some of the issues surrounding choice in primary care, and recommend how choice can be developed in the most equitable way.

Choice of GP

Removing registration; free choice of GP

Offering absolute choice of GP would replicate systems like those in Germany, Belgium and Switzerland where patients are able to access specialists directly, and GPs do not act as gatekeepers. By removing the enforced loyalty of patients, it is theorised that doctors could be more motivated to meet their needs to ensure patients' custom is retained. However, this would have much wider implications for the NHS, which is organisationally and financially based around the GP gatekeeper and registered population. Removing registration would also make practice-based commissioning impossible, and remove any existing motives for population health management and prevention. Patients are not used to self-referral to specialists, and without professional advice over-use and under-use of specialist services could result. Comparative research has also shown that gatekeeping functions do not have a very significant impact on doctor-patient relationships (van den Brink-Muinen et al, 2003).

Removing registration would also reduce continuity of care. Continuity of care is highly valued by patients, leading to increased satisfaction and trust, reduced complaints and litigation, more appropriate utilisation of resources and better health outcomes (Primary Care Expert Task and Finish Group, 2003). It is also worth noting that traditionally non-gatekeeper European health systems are now introducing forms of gatekeeping, for example in Germany where patients are financially incentivised to consult a GP before going to a specialist. This is largely in order to control healthcare inflation caused by rising consumer demand in a non-gatekeeper, decentralised social insurance system.

Although it is unlikely that the registration system will be removed altogether, there may be elements of liberalisation that could be implemented in order to achieve benefits of responsiveness and personalisation.

Reducing geographical restrictions

The current system of restricting patients by geographical area restricts choice and is inequitable for patients in areas with poor levels or quality of GP services. Liberalising the practice boundary system could in the short term bring benefits to patients in areas with poor levels of provision. By allowing patients to register with a GP outside their area, patients could be freed up from under-provision or poor quality provision to access GP practices further afield. To an extent this already happens, with PCTs allocating patients facing closed lists to alternative providers.

Reducing geographical restrictions could also carry risks. Not all patients are equally able or willing to exercise choice so choice of GP could lead to sink services in some areas. GPs' links with local communities could be threatened, and by having registered patients from further afield practices would be less able to manage their local population's health. Therefore commissioners need to ensure that existing providers improve and new providers enter the market where there is under-provision.

Registration currently disadvantages particularly socially excluded groups who may move around more or have no fixed abode, including homeless people, people in temporary accommodation, Travellers/Gypsies and migrants. At present registration is reactive, with patients only joining a practitioner's list when they go to the surgery and fill in a form. More proactive mechanisms could be used to ensure that transient groups are registered with a primary care practice. For example, registering patients according to Office for National Statistics census lists has been suggested. However, alternative datasets also suffer from shortcomings of survey techniques, as the under-estimates of the population in the 2001 census showed.

Involvement of other public services and the Voluntary and Community VCS could help ensure that potentially excluded patients are registered. For example, homeless projects could also provide information and support on health issues and help people to register with a GP. The homeless organisation Broadway helps clients register with GPs, gives them information on their rights and supports them if registration is refused. As more diverse types of practice are developed, these could include practices specialising in hard to reach groups, perhaps being based in or providing outreach services in homeless hostels, Traveller communities or immigration advice services. Access to choice should be particularly targeted at excluded groups so that their needs and preferences can be met, and their voices can be heard.

Convenience

Choice of GP has also been proposed to improve ease of access for people with commitments that make it more difficult for them to access GPs. Easing geographical restrictions could improve convenience of access, for example for people with work commitments that mean they are less able to see a GP during the day. This could reduce healthcare inequities because lower socio-economic groups tend to have less accommodating work patterns, being paid by the hour or on short-term contracts that make appointments difficult (Dixon et al, 2003).

The NHS should allow people to register with two practices, one at home and one near their place of work, or near a relative or friend, including informal carer. This would be facilitated by electronic care records, allowing GPs to share information about patients. This could have a number of benefits, including less delayed access for people with commitments; more appropriate care and improved health; reduced non-attendance at appointments; work days saved; and staff morale improved. Commissioners would have to ensure that expansion of services in employment centres was based on the health needs of people working in that area. In particular, PCTs would need to ensure that resources were not further diverted away from poor areas with lower provision according to need in order to pay higher rents and overheads in business districts. People working in lower paid and less flexible jobs should be targeted for flexible dual registration, with extra advice and information to encourage them to choose this service.

Other options to improve convenience might be for some practices to offer more accessible appointments outside normal working hours. A survey for the BBC found that 45 per cent of GPs thought standards of out of hours care had dropped since the new contract (BBC, 2005c), while 21 per cent of patients in the national survey of patients said they were sometimes or often deterred from going to their general practice because of inconvenient opening hours (Healthcare Commission, 2005). However, where practices have introduced longer opening hours, as in one east London practice, the '8 'til 8 team' has seen its practice expand as patients choose to move to their more accessible service. The minority ethnic and immigrant community organisation ATD 4th World told us that more flexible GP appointments need to fit in with people's busy lives. Families in crisis worry about missing appointments. This demonstrates the demand for more flexible opening hours, a demand that GPs are currently not meeting. Other service sectors, for instance in retail and schools, have expanded out-of-hours services.

Choice is one way to break down monopolies and increase the incentives for GP practices to provide more public-focused services in the community, rather than call centres or inefficient use of accident and emergency departments. PCTs or practices could provide non-doctor services from the GPs' premises, for example nurse and therapist-led services, to continue beyond the working hours of GPs, providing 'wrap-around' primary health services. Social needs could also be met out of hours, for example by Citizens Advice advocates or community organisations supporting people to access information and make choices.

GPs could also be hired through locum or commercial contracts, bringing in more flexible services and creating more competitiveness, to increase efficiency and create the 'grit in the oyster', as treatment centres have in secondary care. This could create the incentives for existing GPs to offer more patient-centred opening hours. For disadvantaged and under-provided patients, more customer-focused GP services would reduce the barriers to access caused by inconvenient opening hours and inconsistent quality.

Creating specialism and appropriate treatment

One likely effect of creating more choice of GP is an increased sorting of patients. Currently, registered patients are meant to be drawn fairly representatively from the local practice area. Allowing patients to choose practices further away, and encouraging a wider range of providers, would encourage practices to develop specialisms to attract patients of a certain demographic or health group.

Specialisation would offer more meaningful choice for patients than just choice of family GPs. The traditional model of 'family services' is difficult to maintain, sustained more by professional tradition than patient-centred policies. Rather than choosing from a range of providers offering the same one-size-fits-all services, patients could choose a provider that met their specific cultural, age and health needs. So choice could allow patients to access a wider range of more personalised services, building on the successes of GPs with a Special Interest. For example, patients could choose to register at a practice that can provide GPs for particular ethnic and cultural needs, including multilingual GPs; adolescent specialist practices could be developed, as could family practices or practices specialising in services for older people.

Primary care commissioning networks

Networks of specialist practices could develop by collaborating and pooling practice-based commissioning budgets. A network of commissioning practices would be able to refer to other specialist GPs within the commissioning collaborative. Registration with an individual GP would offer an entry into a network of commissioning practices offering a range of specialisms, opening times and locations.

Encouraging specialisation and segmentation could also provide opportunities for providers to break down barriers between primary and secondary care. A collaborative of primary care practices could commission consultants in the community, either employed by them or commissioned from other providers including foundation trusts. Specialist GPs could provide services that are more traditionally hospital outpatients-based, including screening. This would contribute to the government's aim to shift care out of hospitals closer to the community to meet patients' needs and to improve efficiency.

Where patients are referred within primary care networks, for example a GP referring a patient to a local practice with a sexual health specialist service (which may be GP- or nurse-led), cross charging or budget pooling should be used to ensure that money follows the patient's choice.

There are drawbacks to encouraging specialisation, particularly if it goes as far as niche provision or carve-outs – providers specialising in a particular niche health group. People with complex co-morbidities could pose a challenge to the model of specialist primary care. Specialisation could also damage the principle of holistic, whole patient centred care and continuity. Carve-outs would be more suited to the top two or three conditions that are a particular problem in an area (NHS Alliance, 2004). For example, an area with high incidence of diabetes could have a specialist diabetes provider with particular expertise in the health needs of people with that condition. Demographic specialism, rather than medical specialism, could be preferable to encourage social and person-centred care, rather than treating patients as a set of symptoms or labelled as 'diabetic' or 'heart condition'.

We recommend that, whilst a patient will be encouraged to choose and register with a 'first-stop' GP to be their gatekeeper, care co-ordinator and representative in the health system, GPs would no longer be the sole primary care doctor that a patient would see. First-contact GPs would be able to refer patients within primary care to another practice within an integrated primary care network.

With less geographical constraint on choice, and greater segmentation and specialisation, inevitably GPs will serve patients from a wider area. There is a concern that this could weaken doctors' local community ties, and reduce incentives to manage the health of their population. However, this model would also provide opportunities for patients to access a wider range of primary care services in the community and provide wider opportunities for patients to be engaged in choice and collective voice. PCTs would still have responsibility to assess population health needs.

Increasing the scope of choice of GPs would incentivise practices to involve patients collectively in commissioning and service decisions. If local community and voluntary groups support disadvantaged patients in accessing information and making choices, as discussed in chapter three, practices will be able to involve these organisations in setting priorities and designing services to meet local needs. Therefore these policies could create a more powerful role for community and voluntary groups in local health decision-making.

A wider range of more specialist opportunities in the community could help tackle recruitment and retention problems, and improve service levels in under-provided areas. Opportunities for new roles, incorporating aspects of secondary and primary care, would be attractive to GPs. For example, the London Assembly recommended a new role of 'portfolio GP' to attract younger doctors to work part time as GPs in under-provided areas, with the flexibility to undertake work in secondary care, the community and research (London Assembly Health Committee, 2003). Other health workers within more specialist practices, including primary care nurse practitioners and first contact allied health professionals, could take on key worker and gatekeeping functions traditionally limited to GPs (NHS Alliance, 2004).

Maintaining continuity of care and family services
Progressive choice in primary care, with more specialism and segmentation to meet the needs of diverse groups more appropriately, should not mean that GPs' traditional roles would be lost. As discussed, gatekeeping, co-ordination and continuity of care are valued features of primary care. 'Traditional' generic family practices should still exist, alongside specialist and segmented options.

It should be recognised that some patients – particularly families and possibly older people – will want to stay with a generic practice. This will remain a valid choice, and in effect family healthcare will become a specialism again. Whichever doctor or practice patients register with, much of their budget will be pooled within local primary care networks to commission appropriate care in the community or at hospital. Therefore generic

GPs, including single-handed practices, will be able to co-exist with more specialist providers, if patients choose. Their patients will, however, have access to a wider range of services in the community at larger polyclinics or specialist practices.

Where there is segmentation, it should be managed so that care is joined-up and seamless (NHS Alliance, 2004). Within a more complex networked primary care service, care pathway co-ordination will be a more important function for all GPs. When collaborating to commission services for particular conditions, primary care professionals will have to think about the pathway of care from a patient's perspective. Rather than leaving it to the individual to negotiate fragmented services, the onus will be on commissioners to specify the pathway. For patients with more complex needs, GPs and other professionals will have to guide patients, supporting them to make choices along the way. Service navigation will become a more important skill in primary care as the emphasis shits to commissioning and providing choices of treatments in the community. Patient groups in the community and voluntary sector will have a role to play in supporting patients to navigate their pathway.

Incentivising performance and responsiveness

One of the aims of progressive choice is to be more responsive to patients' needs. We recommend that the policy aim should be to increase variety so that a wider range of services is available and patients can access the care the need, at the time and place they prefer. Commissioners should aim to improve contestability, for example by injecting spare capacity, providing quality information and transport support. However the degree of contestability between different providers of the same service will sometimes be limited. For example, for less common specialisms there may be fewer providers from which to choose, with some local monopolies. If providers are not competing directly on quality, there would need to be other mechanisms to drive improvement, including financial incentives, regulation and patient and public involvement.

Challenges for implementing choice in primary care

In theory, there is nothing to stop practices from specialising in particular cultural, demographic or health groups. GPs with a Special Interest have been developed; Alternative Primary Medical Services (APMS) contracts are available for PCTs to use; GPs specialising in minority languages are available in some communities. Much of the legislative and organisational mechanisms to allow choice to be developed in primary care are already in place, but the potential has not been realised. Central government therefore has had to stimulate innovation, for example the Department of Health is providing central support to PCTs to recruit new providers. Primary care needs to reach a point where PCTs, GPs and other providers are incentivised to increase the range of choices themselves. At present, the financial incentives against specialisation and segmentation may be preventing more appropriate and efficient services from being developed locally.

Increased sorting and 'segmentation' of the population would undermine the current funding system for primary care. Under the new General Medical Services (nGMS) contract, practices are funded according to the number of patients on their registers. This is weighted according to the expected average health needs of the wards in which their patients reside. Therefore practices are compensated for the expected costs of their patients, but only if their patients are representative of their ward. The capitation payment is supplemented by the voluntary Quality and Outcomes Framework (QOF) performance, which rewards practices for the provision of quality care, and helps to fund further improvement in the delivery of clinical care.

Almost half of practices are funded under the Primary Medical Services contract, which allows PCTs directly to employ GPs, particularly in areas where there is under-provision by independent contractors under nGMS. Most nGMS practices have opted out of the new capitation formula and are funded according to historic patterns.

If patients were segmented to different practices according to cultural, demographic or health needs then the financing system for primary care would need to be reformed. We therefore propose that the policy for paying GPs by capitation should be revised. Financing primary care by registration and capitation should incentivise population health improvement and manage demand. However, this incentive has not been strong enough in the past. The principle for funding general practice, as with the rest of primary care, should be on health need. As GP and primary care service usage is not equitable, basing GP payments on historic treatment costs effectively perpetuates inequity. GPs should move towards being financed on the basis of patients' needs.

The vision of primary care outlined above allows meaningful choice to be provided to patients that goes beyond simply choice of traditional family GP. By developing a wider range of primary care practices and offering more specialist services to people based on their characteristics and health needs, patients will be able to choose services outside hospital through their GP. New reforms in primary care, including practice-based commissioning, should allow more services to be offered in primary care. Developing choice in community services should lead to an increase in service provision and improved quality.

More detailed work on how commissioning can be used to improve health and reduce health inequalities will be forthcoming from ippr.

If more choice is developed in primary care, then the lessons from choice in secondary care should be applied to improve equity and achieve wider aims of a progressive choice policy. The aim of progressive choice should be to maximise the opportunity to choose, rather than allowing a small minority of mobile and active patients to dominate the market and benefit from voice and navigation skills. As we recommended in chapter two, patient-centred information on access and quality would have to be provided in a range of formats, with support to help disadvantaged groups make informed choices. The VCS should be engaged to support patients and provide them with advice and advocacy to navigate the health system and make healthier choices in their life, including self-care.

Information about choice of GP would include a range of practical and quality indicators. National research on information needs in primary care shows that people want better information about practices, especially what services are available and how to access them (NPCRDC, 2005). Quality measurement in primary care is even less developed than in secondary care because GPs do not provide the same service to all patients in the same way that surgeons perform similar operations. However, there should be better opportunities to measure performance in general, for example results of patient surveys should be published at practice level to inform patients' choices and hold practices accountable.

Practices are now performance monitored using the QOF, where GPs have volunteered to apply for funding rewards based on achievements of certain standards within four domains:

- The clinical domain (76 indicators in 11 areas, for example coronary heart disease or mental health)

- The organisational domain (56 indicators in five areas, for example patient communication or practice management)

- The patient experience domain (four indicators in two areas, patient surveys and consultation length)

- The additional services domain (ten indicators in four areas, including cervical screening or maternity services)

This information was first made public in 2005, and performance of every participating practice can be viewed at http://www.ic.nhs.uk/services/qof/. However, this data is currently unsuitable for informing patient choice. In the contract negotiations, GPs ensured that the QOF would not be used for performance management, but would be a voluntary scheme. Practices have a degree of choice about the measures that are used to assess them, so information is not comparable. The QOF results are published online in a series of spreadsheets that have to be downloaded. Practice names have to be looked up on another spreadsheet, and the score definitions have to be looked up on a separate 18-page table. No information on quality is published on the main www.nhs.uk website, which only shows practical information to inform choice of GP. At present, therefore, there is no useful quality information on which to base choice in primary care.

Our main recommendation for equitable choice of GP is therefore to implement an 'information revolution' in primary care. The government's current information strategy emphasises the need for personal health information and information for choice of hospital (DH, 2004b). If choice is going to be opened up in care outside hospitals, the NHS should provide easily available practical and quality information on local GP services. In particular, as choice and segmentation of patients are developed, information on specialism and quality information in that specialism should also be provided. Comparative information should be made available in a range of locations in a range of formats, as discussed in chapter two.

Support for disadvantaged groups in choice in primary care

> 'We already get questions about what services are available. However, we do not have up-to-date information on what services are available. For example, we only just found out about the carers nurse service, but were not involved in designing the service. Similarly, advocacy services were not previously on offer. Then we discovered yesterday that they were. The PCT should involve organisations like the Alzheimer's Society in designing services. This would mean we were up-to-date on services available and would be better able to support people to make choices and access services.
>
> 'We need this information in one place and up-to-date.'
>
> ippr/Health Link interview with Alzheimer's Society branch

Support for patients to make the right choices in primary care should also be provided, including information brokers and advocates. In practice, especially as the divide between secondary and primary care is blurred, information and support will probably be developed and provided the same way for both sectors.

As in secondary care, there will be an important role for the VCS in helping people access information, providing support to make choices, and representing people's needs and preferences to commissioners and providers. ippr and Health Link explored this in the consultation with organisations supporting disadvantaged groups. Whilst it was difficult for people to discuss the abstract idea of choice in primary care, there was a strong message that access to primary care was difficult for excluded groups, and that signposting information for choice could help patients access the right care at the right place at the right time.

Information support and advocacy in primary care – evidence from ippr/Health Link's consultation with community and voluntary groups

CEMVO
- CEMVO helps people who speak languages other than English to access GPs or other primary care professionals who meet their language or cultural needs. This can happen in some inner city areas. For example in one London area GPs with particular language or cultural understanding can work with voluntary sector organisations to provide support and advice. Patients can come in on a particular day for interpreting in a certain language.

Broadway
- Broadway helps homeless people select GPs using the local area service handbook, but needs more local detail on non-mainstream treatments. It accompanies clients to GP appointments if required.

- Broadway has forged effective links with GPs who have become committed to improving services for homeless people.

- As choice is extended, homeless people need to be empowered and supported. They would require health advocates who understand the services and needs of homeless people or people with long-term conditions.

- Broadway would want to develop a peer education training course on choice in healthcare for homeless clients.

FaithRegen
- FaithRegen could accompany clients to the GP and discuss outcomes and implications with them through advocacy.

- They could arrange health 'surgeries' to coincide with ESOL courses. Black and minority ethnic communities are a captive audience; FaithRegen could provide advice there and then.

Sign
- If there were deaf aware GPs and other primary care services then deaf people could be assisted to use these services. Sign could provide trained BSL-using advocates and outreach workers.

Alzheimer's Society
- Alzheimer's Society branches provide advice on how to get better service from GPs. They help and encourage people to ask for what they want and be more assertive in consultations. They may exceptionally go with a client to the GP consultation.

A quasi-market in primary care, with patients more free to choose between providers and payments following the patients' choice, should be well-regulated to prevent provider selection and ensure that disadvantaged groups are not excluded. Patients and the community should be closely involved in regulating the primary care market.

As with choice in secondary care, choice in primary care would need to be accompanied by a growth in capacity. Choice in secondary care has been accompanied by significant investment in capacity and infrastructure (and to a lesser extent information and support). At present, access to a single primary care provider, let alone choice of more than one, is restricted by an under-provided market, particularly in deprived areas. Choice in primary care may not have the supportive financial environment that secondary care has enjoyed. At present some NHS Trusts are experiencing financial difficulties, and financial stability will be a challenge in the new choice and PbR market. The recent record increases in investment in the NHS budget since 2002 are not likely to continue at the same level following the next spending review.

Markets can only work to incentivise consumers if there is some spare capacity so that patients can move around the system without excessive waits or closed lists. At the moment the incentive effect of choice is glued down by enforced loyalty and a lack of GPs in some areas. Rather than empowering patients, more choice in a capacity constrained system could lead to selection by providers, as has happened in the past when 'choice' of school has been introduced.

Therefore the government and the NHS need to ensure that primary care capacity is built up to offer a wider range of choices. In the longer term, better preventative services could improve efficiency, including reducing demand (or slowing down inflation) in secondary care. However, the government will need to consider additional funding for choice in primary care at least in the short term to create incentive effects and a wider range of choices for patients – the equivalent to hospital building and diagnostic and treatment centres in secondary care. If reform in primary care identifies previously unmet need, particularly in disadvantaged groups, assumptions of immediate savings or cash neutrality may be flawed.

Choice for people with long-term conditions

Choice in primary care could potentially offer benefits for people with long-term conditions; in turn, empowering people with long-term conditions could bring major benefits to the health system. However, the current choose and book policy, which is based around creating a market for episodic hospital-based operations, is not based around the needs of people with long-term conditions. Long-term conditions require care by a range of health and social care professionals, with continuity of care, ongoing relationships with carers and local access of critical importance. Choice in long-term conditions is therefore more complex than choice in elective surgery and services are less amenable to marketisation. This section will look at how choice should be developed in order to improve health and wellbeing, particularly for disadvantaged groups.

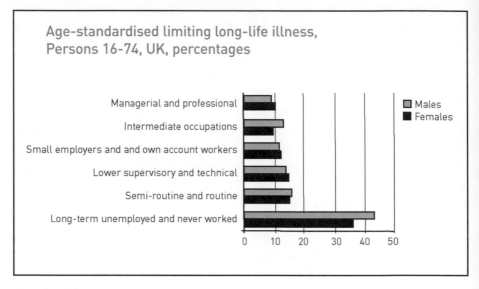

Age-standardised limiting long-life illness, Persons 16-74, UK, percentages

Source: Coulthard et al, ONS, 2004

As discussed in chapter one, whilst average life expectancy has risen, the gap between life expectancy for top and bottom social classes has increased. Long-term conditions have exacerbated this inequality, as the gap in healthy life expectancy between social classes has also increased, so that people living in the most deprived wards in England have a shorter healthy life expectancy than people in least deprived wards, by nearly 17 years for men and women.

	Male life expectancy	Male healthy life expectancy	Female life expectancy	Female healthy life expectancy
Least deprived 10% of wards	77.4	66.2	81.2	68.5
Most deprived 10% of wards	71.4	49.4	78.0	51.7

Source: Bajekal, 2005

At present the NHS and social care system does not meet the needs of people with long-term conditions effectively. For patients and their families, waiting for diagnoses and negotiating with a range of fragmented providers across health and social care can be complicated and stressful, and create barriers to effective care. They have to fit in with how the current care system works rather than using a care system that works for them (NHS Confederation, 2005).

The fact that the health and care system is not designed around complex needs leads to inefficiency and higher costs. People with long-term conditions account for 80 per cent of GP appointments and over 60 per cent of hospital bed days. Unplanned admissions prevent the health system from meeting the targets that government has set, for example leading to surgical cancellations and bed shortages and contributing to the spread of healthcare-acquired infections. The World Health Organisation has identified that long-term conditions will be the leading cause of disability by 2020 and, if not managed, will become the most expensive problem for health systems (DH, 2004d). This challenge has been taken up by the government,, and a national NHS and Social Care Model for managing long-term conditions was published in 2005 (DH, 2005e). However there is a risk that choice policy based on elective surgery will leave long-term conditions as a second priority, below competing for patients under choose and book.

The progressive model of equitable choice in healthcare applies well for people with long-term conditions. People living with a long-term condition can become knowledgeable about their health needs and can take control of their own lives through healthcare choices, self-care and everyday life choices. The government has recognised the potential for self-care across the health system, including prevention and self-treatment for minor ailments, and has developed policies to enable self management of long-term conditions (DH, 2005f). At present, however, the information and skills to self-care and to make the best personal and healthcare choices are not easily available, and there can be particular barriers for people from disadvantaged groups.

A survey found that disadvantaged groups, including the elderly, deprived and ethnic minority groups were least confident in their knowledge and understanding of self-care (DH, 2005b). There is a risk that the proposed model for managing chronic disease in the NHS and social care may be implemented with a top-down approach, identifying patients at risk of unplanned admissions to hospital using predictive modelling to provide a standard disease and case management package without involving the patient in the decisions. Chronic disease management policy may be led too much by hospital cost savings, and less led by values of empowerment and equity. Choice should be used to engage people in their healthcare decisions, improve health literacy and enable people to self-care. If chronic disease management is rationed too much by professional 'experts' then patients might not engage in managing their condition effectively. In particular, patients who are not identified as being high risk and are therefore not provided with the intensive interventions of disease management and case management could degenerate if they are not given opportunities to choose elements of the higher intensity interventions.

Our vision of progressive choice in primary care, accompanied by increasing capacity and diversity of providers outside hospitals, underpinned by better information and support linked to the VCS, could contribute to meeting the challenge of long-term conditions. In particular, specialist primary care providers for people with a particular health need could cater for people with more common long-term conditions. For example, in areas with high diabetic incidence, GPs with a specialism working in practices with expert nurses and support staff could provide joined-up services in the community without the need for referrals to hospital. These GPs would also be able to provide generic services (and have access to a network of other specialist practices) so that the whole person's needs could be met, but their particular expertise would enable more appropriate services to be conveniently available in the community.

For people with long-term conditions, choice of primary care provider could therefore allow them to access more expertise and specialist care outside hospital. However, choice in long-term conditions should also be developed within services. For some people, a more traditional generalist or a cultural or demographic specialist practice might be preferable to a practice specialising in one or two conditions. In less densely populated areas, or for less common conditions, there may not be a relevant specialist available within convenient travelling time (although targeted assistance with transport would help people to reach primary care providers in their network). Even within specialist services, there should be a range of choices to enable patients to personalise their package of care.

As the NHS and social care model for chronic disease management is rolled out, PCTs and primary care practices will have to specify generic care pathways offered for patients with particular long-term conditions. Specified care pathways should provide 'choice points' along the way, so that a patient with a particular condition is enabled to make decisions about their treatments, including provider and locations. The current model proposes personalised care plans for the most vulnerable patients with high risk of hospitalisation. Whilst it may be necessary to focus high intensity interventions on those most at risk, requiring the rest of patients with long-term conditions to fit into a standardised pathway could reduce their engagement with their care and therefore increase their chance of deteriorating to a higher risk. There are more than 300 combinations of drugs, activity, food and monitoring methods that can be tailored to an individual with diabetes (Roberts, 2004). A form of care pathway plan may offer a half-way between individual care planning with a case manager and fitting into a standardised pathway, and could record the choices a patient has made within a flexible care pathway.

Birmingham and The Black Country Strategic Health Authority has examined choice in long-term conditions and has recommended care pathways be developed that offer choices at various stages. Generically, the stages of the pathway include:

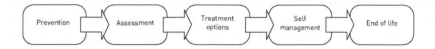

BBCSHA, 2005

Choice in breast cancer services

An example of an important care pathway is in breast cancer services. Because the main priority in cancer services is speed of assessment, with a target of two weeks from referral to assessment for suspected cancer patients, cancer has not been included in secondary care choice policies. Ninety-seven per cent of diagnosed cancer patients begin their treatment within one month, so choice of treatment centres based on waiting times is not critically relevant to cancer. However, in order to involve patients in decision-making and to ensure that services are personalised, more choice needs to be provided along the cancer pathway.

The All Party Parliamentary Group on Breast Cancer (2005) has therefore recommended that patients should be offered choice of breast cancer unit where they will receive diagnostic tests after referral. However, it is important that choice is also offered post-diagnosis, as a patient going for a diagnostic test should not be expected to make a choice of treatment provider before they have been diagnosed. Information on breast cancer centres and surgeons should be provided, including quality and treatment options, as some centres and consultants offer different surgical options.

Information and choice within management of breast cancer should also be provided, including pain management, hair loss and wig services, with appropriate support to make informed choices, including information and support prescriptions to voluntary and community support groups. Choice at end of life should also be provided, as currently people's preferences to die at home are not met.

Plurality of providers for people with long-term conditions could offer patients a wider range of alternative pathways that could meet their preferences. As case management and disease management are rolled out, PCTs will commission organisations from different sectors to provide focused management for individuals and groups to help them manage their condition and avoid unplanned hospital admissions. Our vision for choice in primary care would allow greater specialisation within existing and new providers, with chronic disease management more mainstreamed, so it may be unnecessary to commission large providers of chronic disease management.

PCTs should use their commissioning power to ensure that chronic disease and case management organisations provide choice within their services to patients, and ensure that patients are involved in decision-making. Whilst it will be beneficial to patients not to have to navigate a complex system if they have a niche specialist provider, neither should they have to fit into a set of pre-determined pathways. Patients should also, where practicable, be offered choice between chronic disease management providers, creating contestability and a wider range of options for patients.

Patients with long-term conditions would benefit from a plurality of care pathways. In particular, new pathways should be offered, based on self-management and self-referral. This could provide real autonomy for patients, linking choice with self-care and rights with responsibilities (see box).

Case study of self-referral for IBD

Patients with Inflammatory Bowel Disease (IBD) are normally seen by a specialist in a hospital outpatients department. Their consultant traditionally books an appointment for patients at a regular interval. A trial conducted by the National Primary Care Research and Development Centre provided patient-centred information, a written self-management guide, training for consultants in a patient-centred approach, and the option to self-refer direct to a consultant when patients identified their own needs.

The intervention led to a reduction in consultations and reduced Did Not Attends. The majority of patients in the intervention preferred direct access. Rather than individualising patients as self-seeking consumers, evaluations of this experiment with self-management and direct access to specialists made reference to people expressing collective responsibility when deciding whether to book an appointment with a specialist.

Source: Rogers et al, 2004

The experiment with self-referral for IBD demonstrates how information, self-management and choice can work together to improve appropriateness and effectiveness. The choice to go back to the traditional system of consultant-set appointments was made by a quarter of participants, showing that several pathways can exist side-by-side. The learning from this study could be implemented for other long-term conditions, providing direct access in other ways. For example, informed self-referral to allied health professionals such as physiotherapists could be developed to improve equity and health literacy and self-management of chronic disease (Chartered Society of Physiotherapy, 2004)

As patient choice could lead to more segmentation and specialisation, independent brokers, navigators or advocates could be involved to help patients access information and make choices. Information provision and choice support could be provided by GPs where appropriate. However there needs to be broader thinking about care co-ordinators, involving nurses, information officers and fellow patients. Patients should be signposted to voluntary and community organisations that can provide support and link people with peer groups (Corben and Rosen, 2005). Linking patients with long-term conditions with information and support in the VCS could also help disadvantaged patients achieve more equitable outcomes. Awareness of support groups and voluntary organisations appears to be low, with 68 per cent unaware of any but 66 per cent saying they would be more confident in doing self-care if they had support from people with similar health concerns or conditions (DH, 2005b).

Support from peers to help people manage their long-term conditions more effectively is being actively piloted in the NHS. The expert patients programme has provided lay-taught courses for people with long-term conditions to help them live with chronic illness. This programme is being expanded, whilst other programmes should also be developed as part of the support framework for patient choice outlined in this report, drawing on VCS organisations to provide information and advocacy. A plurality of self-management courses should be funded so that patients can choose a programme that suits their needs, perhaps offering disease-specific, community-based or demographic-based courses. The choice support system we propose would be able to signpost patients to course providers as part of the information brokering role.

Collective choices

As well as individual choice, the increase of long-term conditions creates new communities of patients who, as well as supporting each other through self-management courses, should also become involved with healthcare services. Patients with a long-term condition, particularly in areas where choice between chronic disease management providers is less feasible, should be consulted to help design pathways so that they meet their needs and preferences. The NHS, in partnership with the VCS, should facilitate communities of patients, allowing peer groups to meet in person or virtually. This could help improve their collective knowledge and help people to share information, but would also provide a collective forum for joint decision-making about their services with commissioners and providers. At present this can happen locally where patients can join local patients' organisations such as a cancer support group or a local Mencap branch, but this tends to be patchy and under-resourced. As part of the equitable choices support framework proposed, local networks for long-term conditions should be created that would provide a forum for consultation and collective decision-making as well as brokering information and advocacy for individual choices.

For example, regional cancer networks have been established as the organisational model for delivering the NHS cancer plan. Whilst these are delivery networks, their websites also provide information and signposting to local and national support organisations, although these forums are not publicised to patients when they are first referred or diagnosed. Similar disease-specific networks for other long-term conditions should also be established, with the NHS providing some resources to establish the networks as hubs to provide information and support. These networks could then be used to involve patient communities in collective decision-making about services in their area, bringing together patient choice and collective voice.

Breakthrough Breast Cancer has piloted *Adopting the pledge* with five NHS Trusts. In these pilots, cancer centres adopted between three and twelve targets for improvement, based on approval of the multi-disciplinary team, audits of patients' views, consultation with colleagues and discussion with patients.

The targets from which pledges were selected were under five themes:

- greater patient involvement in their own care

- family and friends support

- greater choice

- improved communication

- faster start to radiotherapy.

The Trusts' individualised 'service pledges' were then written down and provided to patients using the service, raising their awareness of their entitlements and involving them in a collective form of choice. The patient consultations made particular use of cancer user groups and former patients, with patient audits conducted by former patients with current patients.

An initial independent consultant's evaluation found that the pledge is an effective patient-led tool for service improvement, and recommended that good practice be learned for wider roll-out in breast cancer and other cancers and long-term conditions (Wilson, 2004).

Choice provides new rights and requires new responsibilities to be taken by patients. This should not be seen as a 'burden' but as an opportunity, as patients and the public have frequently demonstrated a desire for the opportunity to take more responsibility for their own health. Research carried out for the Department of Health showed that there is an appetite amongst the public to self-care – more than nine in ten people were interested in each of four types of self-care activities (lifestyle, taking care of minor injuries, long-term conditions and following discharge from hospital). However there is a lack of awareness and understanding of what people could be doing. More than half of those who had seen a care professional in the previous six months said they had not often been encouraged to do self-care, and a third said they had never been encouraged by professionals (DH, 2005b). The research concludes that information and knowledge, as well as guidance by professionals and support groups are key factors in increasing self-care behaviour. This particularly impacts on disadvantaged groups who are currently least active in self-care, particularly the most elderly, deprived and minority ethnic groups (DH, 2005b).

Better joining up of self-care initiatives and choice information and support policies could help deliver more equitable choice and better outcomes for disadvantaged groups. When patients are given information on treatment and provider choices, and signposted to sources of information and support in the community, this should include information on self-care and healthy life choices. In particular, patient support organisations and networks of existing patients can provide useful sources of peer information. Patients will often have other health and wider social problems that can be improved using a more whole-person model of information and support.

For example, the expert patient programme provides courses using lay patient tutors to facilitate groups of patients to help them live with and manage chronic disease. Other self-care programmes include DAFNE and DESMOND, structured self-help programmes for people with diabetes; the Health of Men project in Airedale PCT; and pharmacy practices in Tyne and Wear. Information and support for patient choice should include options to enable people to self-manage better and improve their health outcomes, particularly for disadvantaged groups who do not get the most from self-care (DH, 2005f).

Conclusions

Up to now government policy has concentrated on developing choice in secondary care. This could challenge the aim of shifting care from secondary to primary and preventative care.

It is not presently clear what choice means in primary care. From an equity point-of-view, lack of access to primary care can create barriers for patients, particularly those living in areas with closed GP lists or whose GPs have opening hours that are difficult for people with unstable work or caring commitments. Patient transport is not provided for access to primary care. Quality of primary care can also be variable, and patients do not receive equitable treatments or referrals according to need.

Greater choice of GP should be introduced. People with commitments that take them outside their home area should be allowed to register at a secondary practice near their place of work, or near to relatives. However, a greater benefit from increasing choice of GP would be to encourage greater specialisation, either by a particular health need or a demographic group. This vision of primary care could improve the range of services available outside hospital, with networks of commissioning practices collaborating to provide a wider range of traditionally secondary services in the community.

Many of the mechanisms already exist to facilitate this transition. However, the current system for funding GPs is a barrier. At present most GPs are paid a salary or are funded according to historical patterns, rather than on the basis of the health needs of their population. A review of GP funding, currently due, should look more broadly at paying GPs according to the needs of the patients they serve.

There needs to be an 'information revolution' in primary care to match the government's aim to increase information for choice in secondary care. As discussed in chapters two and three, information needs to be backed up with support and advocacy for disadvantaged groups. Voluntary and community organisations should be commissioned to provide this information and to feed back to primary care on the needs and preferences of local people.

People with long-term conditions would be the group most able to benefit from our vision of progressive choice based on empowerment and improving health. However, the current emphasis on choice of hospital does not serve this group's needs. Choice in long-term conditions needs to be developed throughout the pathway of care. A wider range of more specialist commissioners and providers in primary care would improve services for people with long-term conditions, including choice of pathway and choice of disease or case management organisation. Choice could enable and incentivise patients to do more self management.

As well as individual choice, the NHS, in partnership with voluntary and community organisations, should facilitate communities of patients who could support each other and participate in collective choices, strengthening the voice of disadvantaged groups and reversing historic inequities in the NHS.

References

6, Perri (2003) 'Giving consumers of British public services more choice: What can be learned from recent history', *Journal of Social Policy* 32(2)

Acheson, D. (Chairman) (1998) *Independent inquiry into inequalities in health report* London: The Stationery Office

All Party Parliamentary Group on Breast Cancer (2005) 'The future of patient choice: What should it mean to a breast cancer patient?', *Breast Cancer Bulletin* 16

Appleby, J. (2005) 'Impact of choice on hospital viability', *Health Service Journal* 115(5945)

Appleby, J. and Devlin, N. (2005) *Measuring NHS success: Can patients' views on health outcomes help to manage performance?* London: King's Fund

Appleby, J., Harrison, A. and Devlin, N. (2003) *What is the real cost of more patient choice?* London: King's Fund

Audit Commission (2001) *Going places: taking people to and from education, social services and healthcare* London: Audit Commission

Audit Commission (2005) *Early lessons from payment by results* London: Audit Commission

Bajekal, M. (2005) 'Healthy life expectancy by area deprivation: magnitude and trends in England, 1995-1999, *Health Statistics Quarterly* spring, 18-27

Baker, D. and Hann, M. (2001) 'General practitioner services in primary care groups in England: is there inequity between service availability and population need?', *Health and Place* 7(2)

Barber, S. and Gordon-Dseagu, V. (2003) *Equity issues relating to the access and choice programme* London: College of Health

Barber, S., Gordon-Dseagu, V. and Rafferty, J. (2004) *Survey of patients offered choice of hospital in the Greater Manchester area* London: College of Health

Barnes, M. and Prior, D. (1995) 'Spoilt for choice? How consumerism can disempower public service users', *Public Money and Management* July-September

BBC (2005a) 'Reid admits hospitals could close' http://news.bbc.co.uk/1/hi/health/4229791.stm (accessed 24 October 2005)

BBC (2005b) 'NHS use of private sector to rise' http://news.bbc.co.uk/1/hi/health/4542009.stm (accessed 24 October 2005)

BBC (2005c) 'Care "Harmed" by GP night opt-out' http://news.bbc.co.uk/1/hi/health/4295160.stm (accessed 25 October 2005)

Better Regulation Task Force (2005) *Better Regulation for Civil Society*: BRTF

Birmingham and the Black Country Strategic Health Authority (2005) *Choice Delivery Plan* unpublished

Black, D. (Chairman) (1980) *Inequalities in health: Report of a research working group* London: Department of Health and Social Security.

Bridgewater, B. (2005) 'Mortality data in adult cardiac surgery for named surgeons: Retrospective examination of prospectively collected data on coronary artery surgery and aortic valve replacement', *British Medical Journal* 330

Bristol Royal Infirmary Inquiry (2001) *Learning from Bristol: Report of the public inquiry into children's heart surgery at the Bristol Royal Infirmary* London: The Stationery Office

British Medical Association (2004) *British Medical Association written submission to the Public Administration Select Committee Inquiry – Choice and voice in public services* London: British Medical Association

Buchanan, T. (2004) *Defra survey of rural customers; Satisfaction with services* London: Department for Environment, Food and Rural Affairs

Burge, P., Devlin, N., Appleby, J., Rohr, C. and Grant, J. (2005) *London patient choice project evaluation: A model of patients' choices of hospital from stated and revealed preference choice data* Cambridge: RAND Europe

Burgess, S., Propper, C. and Wilson, D. (2005) *Will more choice improve outcomes in education and healthcare? The evidence from economic research* Bristol: Centre for Market and Public Organisation

Byng, S., Farrelly, S., Fitzgerald, L., Parr, S. and Ross, S. (2003) *Having a say: Promoting the participation of people who have communication impairments in healthcare decision-making* London: Department of Health

Catton, H. (2005) 'Introduction', in *Real choice in the Health Service: An RCN discussion document* London: Royal College of Nursing

Chartered Society of Physiotherapy (2004) *Self-referral to physiotherapy services* London: CSP

Citizens Advice (2001) *Unhealthy charges* London: Citizens Advice

Citizens Advice (2004) *'Choosing health': Citizens Advice's response to the Department of Health* London: Citizens Advice

Commission for Health Improvement (2003) *Local health services patient survey 2003* London: Commission for Health Improvement

Commission for Health Improvement (2004) *i2i – Involvement to improvement: Sharing the learning on patient and public involvement from CHI's work* London: Commission for Health Improvement

Commission for Racial Equality (2004) *Gypsies and Travellers: A strategy for the CRE, 2004-7* London: Commission for Racial Equality

Corben, S. and Rosen, R. (2005) *Self-management for long-term conditions: Patient perspectives on the way ahead* London: King's Fund

Coulter, A. (2002) *The autonomous patient: Ending paternalism in medical care* London: Nuffield Trust

Coulter, A., Le Maistre, N. and Henderson, L. (2005) *Evaluation of London patient choice: Patients' experience of choosing where to undergo surgical treatment* Oxford: Picker Institute Europe

Coulthard, M., Yuan, H., Dattani, N., White, C., Baker, A and Johnson, B. (2004) 'Chapter 6: Health' in Babb, P., Martin, J. and Haezewindt, P. *Focus on social inequalities* London: Office for National Statistics

Cowling, J. (2005) 'It's all in the heuristics', *The Journal of Progress* spring 2005

Damiani, M., Propper, C. and Dixon, J. (2005) 'Mapping choice in the NHS: Cross-sectional study of routinely collected data', *British Medical Journal* 330

Davies, W. (2005) *Modernising with a purpose: A manifesto for a digital Britain* London: ippr

Dawson, D., Jacobs, R., Martin, S. and Smith, P. (2005) *Evaluation of the London patient choice project: System wide impacts* York: Centre for Health Economics

Department of Health (2001) *Valuing people: A new strategy for learning disability for the 21st century* London: Department of Health

Department of Health (2003a) *Tackling health inequalities: A programme for action* London: Department of Health

Department of Health (2003b) *Building on the best: Choice, responsiveness and equity in the NHS* London: The Stationery Office

Department of Health (2004a) *Making partnership work for patients, carers and service users: A strategic agreement between the Department of Health, the NHS and the voluntary and community sector* London: Department of Health

Department of Health (2004b) *Better information, better choices, better health: Putting information at the centre of health* London: Department of Health

Department of Health (2004c) *The NHS Improvement Plan: Putting people at the heart of public service* London: The Stationery Office

Department of Health (2004d) *Improving chronic disease management* London: Department of Health

Department of Health (2004e) *Payment by results: DH response to consultation* London: DH

Department of Health (2005a) *Tackling health inequalities: Status report on the programme for action* London: Department of Health

Department of Health (2005b) *Public attitudes to self-care baseline survey* London: Department of Health

Department of Health (2005c) *Choice at six months: Good practice* London: Department of Health

Department of Health (2005d) *Code of conduct for payment by results: Draft for consultation* London: Department of Health

Department of Health (2005e) *Supporting people with long-term conditions: An NHS and social care model to support local innovation and integration* London: Department of Health

Department of Health (2005f) *Self-care – a real choice* London: Department of Health

Dixon, A., Le Grand, J., Henderson, J., Murray, R. and Poteliakhoff, E. (2003) *Is the NHS equitable? A review of the evidence* London: LSE Health and Social Care

Dixon, M. (2004) 'The impact of patient choice on general practice' in Mythen, M. and Coffey, T. (eds) *Patient power: The impact of patient choice on the future NHS* London: New Health Network

Farrell, C. (2004) *Patient and public involvement in health: The evidence for policy implementation* London: Department of Health

Foundation Trust Network (2005) *NHS foundation trusts… Making a difference* London: Foundation Trust Network

Hart, J. (1971) 'The inverse care law', *Lancet* 405(12)

Healthcare Commission (2005) *State of healthcare 2005* London: HC

Health Link (2004) *Taking soundings: Patient and public involvement in the London patient choice project – testing the views of patients including 'hard to reach' groups* London: Health Link

Health Service Ombudsman for England (2004) *Annual report 2003-04* London: The Stationery Office

Help the Aged (2003) *Fair for all, personal to you: choice, responsiveness and equity in the NHS and social care – the Help the Aged response* London: Help the Aged

Hewitt, P. (2005) Speech by Rt Hon Patricia Hewitt MP, Secretary of State for Health, 23 June: Britain speaks

Hibbard, J., Slovic, P., Peters, E., Finucane, M. and Tusler, M. (2001) 'Is the informed-choice policy approach appropriate for Medicare beneficiaries?', *Health Affairs* 20(3)

Hibbard, J., Stockard, J. and Tusler, M. (2003) 'Does publicising hospital performance stimulate quality improvement efforts?', *Health Affairs* 22(2)

Klein, R. (2003) 'A Comment on Le Grand's Paper from a Political Science Perspective' in Oliver, A. (ed.) *Equity in health and healthcare: views from ethics, economics and political perspective: Proceedings from a meeting of the Health Equity Network* London: The Nuffield Trust

Le Grand, J. (2003) *Motivation, agency and public policy. Of knights, knaves, pawns and queens* Oxford: Oxford University Press

Le Grand, J. (2004) *Choice, voice and the reform of public services*, annual lecture of LSE Health and Social Care, 9 December 2004

Le Maistre, N., Reeves, R. and Coulter, A. (2004) *Patients' experience of CHD choice* Oxford: Picker Institute Europe

Lent, A. and Arend, N. (2004) *Making choices. How can choice improve local services?* London: New Local Government Network

London Assembly Health Committee (2003) *GP recruitment and retention: The crisis in London* London: Greater London Authority

Long-term Medical Conditions Alliance (2003) *Fair for all, personal to you: choice, responsiveness and equity in the NHS and social care – Consultation response* London: Long-term Medical Conditions Alliance

Maltby, P. and Gosling, T. (2004) 'Opening it up: Accountability and partnerships' in Gosling, T. (ed.) *3 steps forward, 2 steps back: Reforming PPP policy* London: ippr

Mechanic, D. (1998) 'The functions and limitations of trust in the provision of medical care', *Journal of Health Politics, Policy and Law* 23(4)

Modernising Medical Careers (2005) *Curriculum for the foundation years in postgraduate education and training* London: Modernising Medical Careers

MORI (2003) *Patient choice in Birmingham, Solihull and the Black Country* Birmingham: Birmingham and the Black Country Strategic Health Authority

MORI (2005a) *What does patient choice mean for individual trusts?* presentation to The Real Impact of Patient Choice seminar, 22 April 2005

MORI (2005b) 'Technology Tracker' http://www.mori.com/technology/techtracker. shtml accessed 24 October 2005

National Audit Office (2004) *Choice* Memorandum presented to the Select Committee on Public Administration London: National Audit Office

National Audit Office (2005) *Patient choice at the point of GP referral* London: National Audit Office

National Primary Care Research and Development Centre (NPCRDC) (2005) *Spotlight on: What patients want from primary care* Manchester: NPCRDC

New, B. (1999) 'Paternalism and public policy', *Economics and Philosophy* 15

NHS Alliance (2004) *Choice and access to NHS services: Accessing services provided by allied health professionals and primary care practitioners* Retford: NHS Alliance

NHS Confederation (2003) *Fair for all, personal to you: The NHS Confederation response to the choice consultation* London: NHS Confederation

NHS Confederation (2005) *Our prescription for a healthy NHS* London: NHS Confederation

Office for National Statistics (2005) *National travel survey 2004* London: Department for Transport

Parkinson, J. (2003) *Hearing voices: Negotiating representational claims in public deliberation* Colchester: European Consortium for Political Research

Primary Care Expert Task and Finish Group (2003) *Fair to all personal to you: Recommendations of the Primary Care Expert Task and Finish Group* London: Department of Health

Public Administration Select Committee (2005) *Choice, voice and public services: Fourth report of session 2004-05* London: The Stationery Office

Pyper, C. (2002) 'Knowledge brokers as change agents' in Lissauer, R. and Kendall, L. (eds) *New practitioners in the future health service: Exploring roles for practitioners in primary and intermediate care* London: ippr

Rankin, J. (2005) *A good choice for mental health* London, ippr

Raftery, J. and Harris, M. (2005) *Kidderminster Health: Monitoring and evaluating the reconfiguration of the NHS in Worcestershire* Birmingham: Health Services Management Centre

Reid, J. (2003) Speech by Rt Hon John Reid MP, Secretary of State for Health, 16 July 2003: Choice Speech to the New Health Network.

Roberts, S. (2004) 'The Impact of Patient Choice on Living with a Long-term Condition' in Mythen, M. and Coffey, T. (eds) *Patient power: The impact of patient choice on the future NHS* London: New Health Network

Robinson, J. (2001) 'The end of asymmetric information', *Journal of Health Politics, Policy and Law* 26(5)

Rogers, A., Kennedy, A., Nelson, E. and Robinson, A. (2004) 'Patients' experiences of an open access follow up arrangement in managing inflammatory bowel disease', *Quality and Safety in Healthcare* 13(5)

Saltman, R. (2005) *Primary care in the driver's seat?* London: The Nuffield Trust

Schoen, C., Osborn, R., Huynh, P., Doty, M., Davis, K., Zapert, K. and Peugh, J. (2004) 'Primary care and health system performance: Adults' experiences in five countries' *Health Affairs* Web exclusive

Schwartz, B. (2004) *The paradox of choice: Why less is more* New York: Harper Collins

Segal, L. (1998) 'The importance of patient empowerment in health system reform', *Health Policy* 44(1)

Sihota, S. and Lennard, L. (2004) *Health literacy: Being able to make the most of health* London: National Consumer Council

Social Exclusion Unit (2003) *Making the connections: Final report on transport and social exclusion* London: Office of the Deputy Prime Minister

Social Exclusion Unit (2005) *Improving services, improving lives: Evidence and key themes* London: Office of the Deputy Prime Minister

St George's Healthcare NHS Trust (2005) 'St George's publishes cardiac death rates' press release 14 February 2005 http://www.stgeorges.nhs.uk/press043.asp (accessed 24 October 2005)

Stevens, S. (2003) 'Equity and Choice: Can the NHS offer both? A policy perspective' in Oliver, A. (ed.) *Equity in health and healthcare: views from ethics, economics and political perspective: Proceedings from a meeting of the Health Equity Network* London: The Nuffield Trust

Taylor R., Pringle M. and Coupland C. (2004) *Implications of offering 'patient choice' for routine adult surgical referrals* London: Department of Health

The Guardian 16 March 2005 'Hospitals deny patients facts on death rate'

Thomson, S. and Dixon, A. (2004) 'Choices in healthcare: The European experience', *Euro Observer* 6(4)

Treasure, T. (2005) 'Mortality in adult cardiac surgery: Named surgeon's outcomes have arrived', *British Medical Journal* 330

Vallance-Owen, A., Cubbin, S., Warren, V. and Matthews, B. (2005) 'Outcome monitoring to facilitate clinical governance; Experience from a national programme in the independent sector', *Journal of Public Health* 26(2)

Valuing People Support Team (2005) *The story so far… Valuing People* London: Department of Health

van den Brink-Muinen, A., Verhaak, P., Bensing, J., Bahrs, O., Deveugele, M., Gask, L., Mean, N., Leiva-Fernandez, F., Perez, A., Messerli, V., Oppizzi, L. and Peltenburg, M. (2003) 'Communication in general practice: Differences between European countries', *Family Practice* 20(4)

Wanless, D. (2002) *Securing our future health – Taking a long-term view* London: HM Treasury

Wanless, D. (2004) *Securing good health for the whole population: Final report* London: HM Treasury

Wheeler, B., Shaw, M., Mitchell, R. and Dorling, D. (2005) 'The relationship between poverty, affluence and area' in *Findings* 0425, York: Joseph Rowntree Foundation

Which? (2005) *Which choice?* London: Which?

Wilkinson, R. (2005) *The impact of inequality: How to make sick societies healthier* London: Routledge

Wilson, J. (2004) *Adopting the pledge: A tool for service improvement – evaluation of a pilot project undertaken with breast units in six NHS Trusts in 2004* London: Breakthrough Breast Cancer